The Times

A Biblical view of truth, justice, and hope through examination of where we are, and what is to come.

D0942963

Bobby E. Erickson

The Times

A Biblical view of truth, justice, and hope through examination of where we are, and what is to come.

By Bobby E. Erickson

Bobby E. Erickson

Author Name: Bobby E. Erickson
Visit my LinkedIn website at:
https://www.linkedin.com/in/bobbyeerickson/

Printed in the United States of America

First Printing: January 2021
Kindle Direct Publishing / amazon.us

ISBN-13: 9798587883758
Imprint: Independently published

Dedicated to the many Christians that have stood firm in their faith to share the Gospel message of Jesus Christ. May you find refreshment, encouragement, and empowerment to continue to rescue hearts for His Kingdom, and for His glory...

Prologue

New Believers (also referred to as 'young' Christians) can be very intimidated, even confused, by the language, descriptions, and references used through biblical prophecy. Mature (or seasoned) Believers can lose interest if the information shared doesn't dig deep enough into the details. As a student of Christian theology, teacher, mentor and coach, I try to present information in a way that satisfies many levels of understanding, with focus on the truth.

My hope is that any person reading this book can gain some perspective of possible scenarios we may face in the End Times. Ideally, this would inspire personal study, as well as discussions with others to challenge individual thoughts on this topic. If questions come up, I would strongly suggest talking to a more seasoned Christian that you trust. One simple question may start a wonderful study together; digging deep into the Bible for the truth (John 14:6, 18:37).

Truth, is the Gospel (good news) message of personal salvation made available to everyone, through the finished work of Jesus Christ on the Cross of Calvary (Romans 6:6). If you have not accepted Jesus as your personal Lord and Savior, please open up a discussion with your parents, pastor, or church leadership. It is the true meaning of life.

The hope that comes from understanding and accepting that truth...
is truly endless.

May you be blessed today and always.
Bobby E. Erickson

Acknowledgements

I want to personally thank so many people that have promoted my efforts to chase my dreams.

My wife, Linda, who has always made our home and our children her life's work. I can't remember even one time that she said she was not able to take the reins of our household to allow me time for my pursuits. She is an amazing woman of faith, wife, mother and friend to many.

Logan and Joslyn, my two wonderful kids. They have seen me change hats so many times through the day, that I'm sure their heads are spinning. But through all of that, they continue to show me respect as their father (with an occasional joke here and there, of course). Linda and I are so proud of the young adults they have become, and that they continue to stay true to our family values.

Family is very important, and that extends to our siblings and in-laws as well. Not only have they offered encouragement, but also time to review some of my writing and offer feedback. My Dad and Mom always promoted that we are each unique, but we are all here for each other. Our family lives that out every single day!

The church body has been ever encouraging, also offering time to review my writing and offer feedback. I thank God that I am so blessed to have this fellowship (multiple congregations) to reach out to for prayers and personal care for our family.

Kindle Direct Publishing (KDP) staff. As a first time author, I have needed guidance...no, I needed outright direction! The entire staff has been amazing to work with; inspiring me me achieve my vision for this project vs. telling me 'they can't do that'. They've been a true blessing and such an incredible resource.

Editors and proofreaders. As everyone can imagine, literary work that is going to be published needs extra eyes to review the work. I have been truly blessed to have such a great team of people offering their time and efforts toward this book. There were several areas that were not clear, spelling, grammatical errors, etc. Sometimes I would simply receive a question mark to say "review this", which led to a few re-writes. ALL were appreciated!

I'm sure you can appreciate that there are different views about the End Times, as well as many biblical prophecies. I welcome differing points of view, with the caveat that they point to scripture to back their theory. This led to a few really good discussions on various topics, and promoted clarity in my explanations.

I want to offer a very special thank you to each of the following people for their work, and for being transparent and truthful in their review:

Linda Erickson
Kathy Kuhlmann
James Bolin
Jon Yingling
Shelly Yingling
Pastor Nathan Brand

Table of Contents

Bobby E. Erickson

Chapter 1:
Prophecy, Predestiny and Free will

W hy do we study the End Times? Jesus stated in Matthew 24:42, "Watch therefore, for you do not know what hour your Lord is coming." This message was so important that He restated it again in Matthew 25:13. It can create a bit of confusion, because even if we watch, the signs will not tell us the time nor day of His return (Mark 13:32). So then, why watch? And what are we supposed to be watching for? Are we 'bad' Christians if we don't watch? These are great questions (and valid), and hopefully we can get some clarity on those as we proceed.

The topic we are speaking of is referred to as 'The End Times', or as His Disciples referred to it, "Your (Jesus's) coming (return), and of the end of the age" (Matthew 24:3). The study of the End Times is referred to as Eschatology, and has been the intrigue of many Biblical scholars since the time of Christ. In short, this is trying to figure out the prophetic events (future) that God has stated will occur.

Now, before we try to break down the future, we should also try to understand how we got to where we are today. Why? By understanding the past, we can start to build a timeline of events, show patterns, track what prophecies are fulfilled, or will be fulfilled, and better understand the symbolism that is scattered through prophecies (the Apocalyptic Writings) regarding the End Times.

Eschatology does not affect personal salvation!

Let's start by getting that earlier question answered right away. You are NOT a 'bad' Christian if you do not pursue, or even enjoy, the study of the End Times. This also does not affect your Salvation. You are saved by Grace, through your faith and not of your own works (actions). This is the consistent message throughout the Holy Bible (both Old Testament (Isaiah 64:5) and New Testament (John 3:16, Ephesians 2:8-9)). Salvation changes the heart, which drives actions to produce 'fruit' in life (Galatians 5:22-23).

"For God so loved the world, that He gave His only begotten Son, that whosoever believeth in Him, should not perish, but have everlasting life." - John 3:16

That said, there is an interesting point to consider. It should be noted that God states that the prophecy of Revelation is to be preserved as it was inspired by God to the author, the disciple John (Revelation 22:18-19). In addition, God makes it clear there is blessing to those that hear and maintain the teachings within the book of Revelation (Revelation 1:3, 22:7). Therefore, if you are not interested in studying Eschatology, I would recommend sitting down with a mature Christian who is interested. There is a great hope in studying the fulfillment of God's justice on sin, and the Father of Lies, Satan (John 8:44), as well as the eternal destination within the new Jerusalem for His faithful followers (Revelation 21-22).

Why is prophecy so important?

Is prophecy all about knowing the future? That sounds a little arrogant, doesn't it? Yes, and it can turn into arrogance if the knowledge becomes a source of pride (Proverbs 11:2). This brings up another point regarding the claim of 'knowing' the future. When we interpret prophecy, it is based on our limited (human) understanding; therefore, always verify views with mature Christians and within scripture itself (Proverbs 27:17).

There are some things that are (for the most part) mutually agreed on within theological circles, while others differ based on interpretation of scripture. Timing, allegoric meaning, who or what specific items or figures represent, where events happen, who is or is not involved, etc; all can vary depending on the view of the reader. This is a key point to remember when speaking about the End Times with another person.

Prophecies also add credibility to scripture. This is one reason it is important to understand the events of history; they align to confirm with Prophecy in scripture. Be warned: This is no small task. There are roughly 2,500 prophecies throughout the Bible, and nearly 2,000 of them have been fulfilled. The remaining 500 are either being fulfilled, or will be fulfilled in the End Times. There are many books dedicated to the details and fulfillment of each biblical prophecy.

From a credibility standpoint, the key factors are how precisely each prophecy is fulfilled, and the probabilities associated with each fulfilled prophecy. Consider that we have 2,000 of these incredible prophecies precisely fulfilled, and that the prophecies are from writings that are nearly 2,000 years old. What kind of odds does that create?

Peter Stoner, Chairman of the Mathematics and Astronomy Departments at Pasadena City College, took that challenge head-on in a book called *Science Speaks*. He presented amazing findings based on scientific calculations and probabilities from the facts we know and understand. For example: Stoner showed eight prophecies regarding the Messiah, and found the probability of those coming true (exact in detail) was one in 100,000,000,000,000,000 (this is a hundred quadrillion). We also have to consider this was only .0032% of the total prophecies in the Bible. WOW!

Hugh Ross, President and Founder of Reasons To Believe (RTB), also reviewed the prophecies as a whole, asking the probability that all of these could be fulfilled by chance. His results show the odds of fulfillment without any error is less than one in 10^{2000} - that is a one with 2,000 zeros after it!

This seems to point to something greater than human capacity or understanding. It literally throws most earthly probabilities out the window. Accepting this reality tends to create some intrigue regarding the 500 prophecies that have yet to be fulfilled. Even if we don't understand how soon they will happen, we can attempt to wrap our heads around the impact they will have on humanity and the world we live in.

Is prophecy the same as predestiny?

This is a great question, and one that also creates a lot of discussion in theological circles. One group argues that if everything is predestined by God, then we are simply puppets and our response is already determined by God (no free will). The other side says that God allows us to make our own decisions (free will) - He can intercede as He desires, and already knows the choices we will make. I fall into the second group, and I'll explain why I personally believe it falls in line with teachings of the Bible.

We tend to view time by human standards, and forget that God does not see time the same way we do (2 Peter 3:8). God is omniscient, meaning He knows all things: past, present, future and is everywhere at once. That can be a very hard concept to swallow, but it does help us to understand that God is truly outside of time. The cycle of day and night were created by God in the beginning (Genesis 1:5); man took it from there.

Calendars were invented by humans based on understanding at that time; thus, they vary as well. It is also important to note that historical calendars tracked days, months, years, etc. differently than we do today. Tracking backwards from our current calendar affects months, and even years of biblical dates. This is also key when determining prophecy fulfillment. Hours of the day were also counted a little different in biblical times than we do today, which adds further complexity.

Let's start with a high level review of some differences...

The first calendars are believed to be 'lunar', developed by Egyptians in the 19th Century B.C. These were 30-day calendars, with an additional six days added every 4th year (which is where we get "leap year"). The Jewish people are believed to have created their calendar in the mid-15th Century B.C., with the giving of the law to Moses on Sinai after the Exodus from Egypt. We see evidence of this calendar in the books of Exodus, Leviticus, etc. where months are named specifically.

The Julian calendar (Julius Caesar) was introduced on January 1, 45 B.C. This calendar restored 90 days that were missing from previous calendars, which produced that starting date (1/1). It is believed to be the most accurate calendar that we can use, only varying roughly 10-11 minutes every 128-130 years. That's a lot to take in, but I share that to help understand that the dates, days, months, and even years mentioned are important and can skew historical events or prophecy if not understood. That was a brief history of how we got our current calendar, and some insight regarding the differences between each calendar.

So, how can we explain God's omnipotence in a way that makes sense to us today? Well to start, it's easy for us to understand that God knows all of history; it has already happened, right? But do you realize the future has already happened for God as well (Ecclesiastes 3:15)? This is a common point of contention when considering free will vs. predestiny. Is it possible they are complimentary instead of contradictory (Matthew 19:26)?... How?

It seems we either have free will, or everything is predestined. How can we explain God's omnipotence in a way that makes sense to us as humans?

Free will explained

Picture if you will... You are walking alone in a labyrinth. There is enough light to see the path, and the choices you have to proceed - forward, backward, left, or right. The walls extend well into the open sky, and you can step forward or backward until you come to a 'T'. It's decision time; you need to decide whether to go left or right. Both ways are at least partially lit, so you have some idea of what you are stepping into with either choice. You decide which direction you will go, and you step forward. You may interact with others also placed in the labyrinth, depending on your choices, as well as theirs.

This is the human life. The labyrinth represents all of human time, and you are simply walking through it as one of the billions of humans that have ever lived. Each human being has the free will to decide which direction they will pursue, and what they will not pursue.

Now, picture yourself being a different person: So large that you can see the labyrinth, in its entirety. At the beginning of the labyrinth, you create the first person (Adam), and then create the second (Eve). You can see each individual decision that is made through their entire life as their offspring journey through the labyrinth.

You have the power to add or remove walls or obstacles within the labyrinth (controlling events) at will. It is your choice to either step in and force a situation (Acts 9: 1-19), or simply allow them to choose (Genesis 2-3). This is the view of God over His creation (past, present, future), and His freedom to intercede as He desires.

This is free will. The Bible is full of examples of God (Exodus 32:7-14, 30-35; 33:1-6, 12-17, etc.) and His people (Deuteronomy 28:15, Jonah 1:1-17, etc.) making choices.

Predestiny explained

Predestination means that there is a future event that has already been determined. No matter what we do, that event will occur as it is predestined to occur. To some, if God enforced predestined outcomes, then our choices or actions really don't make any difference. In other words, humans are just God's puppets, and He is making all decisions for us which we are 'claiming' to be free will.

In the previous section, I demonstrated some (and there are MANY more) situations in which God has repented, intervened, or allowed humans to not obey, and take actions based on their own choices. Therefore, we do have free will. So, what about the verses that specifically show God has predestined some things?

I fully believe God *HAS* predestined some things. Just like a lateral in football says it has to go backward, it doesn't state it has to be tossed underhand or overhand, right? It is the same with those things God has predestined. Let's look at a few key points that are backed by scripture:

(1) Free will. God predestined to give free will to human beings, but also to angels. This is documented when Lucifer chose to rebel against God, and he convinced 1/3 of the angels to follow with him in that rebellion (Revelation 12:3-9). Jonah disobeyed God (Jonah 1:3), Joseph and Mary disobeyed God's messenger (an angel of the Lord - Matthew 2:19-23), and many more.

(2) Jesus will defeat sin and Satan. He is the way (John 14:6) for humans to defeat the slavery to Satan caused by our choices of sin. Satan will bruise His heel (hurt), but He will bruise (destroy) Satan's head (Genesis 3:14-15). This is listed as two items, because they are accomplished at two different times. Sin is defeated on the Cross of Calvary (John 19:30), as stated by Jesus, 'it is finished' (John 19:30). Satan is later defeated after the final war

on earth (Revelation 20:10). Ultimately this is finalized by God's statement from the new Jerusalem "It is done." (Revelation 21:6).

(3) Time of Tribulation. This has been foretold by the prophet Daniel (Daniel 9:24-27). Jesus offered a chronological order (Matthew 24), but not an exact time or date for the events (Mark 13:32).

(4) Delivery of blessings. God delivered many blessings to His chosen people, but not all of the blessings. The final blessings will fall on Israel during the Millennium when Jesus returns and sets up His Kingdom on earth.

(5) God's Judgement will come. Everyone will give account of their life to Jesus (Romans 14:10-12, 2 Corinthians 5:10). There are actually two judgements: For Believers (BEMA - 1 Corinthians 3:9-15); and for non-Believers (Great White Throne - Revelation 20:11). All will suffer loss, but the latter will be thrown into the Lake of Fire for all eternity (Revelation 20:15).

The End Time events will occur regardless of the actions we take (they are predestined). Jesus is knocking on every person's door (Revelation 3:20) to offer salvation from our sins (Romans 3:23, Colossians 1:13-14). Our free will allows us to decide if we are going to open the door and accept Jesus Christ, the Son of God, as our Lord and Savior (John 3:16), or reject Him and choose the world instead (John 3:19-21). That decision will determine our individual position (circumstance) through all of the predestined events of the End Times; as well as our eternal destination.

Where will you be? That decision is yours alone...

Chapter 2
My start, Dispensations, & Life today

Let's start with how I got into studying God's Word. I have enjoyed each of my walks through the Bible; however, I would suggest that you develop a plan that works for you. For some people, starting at page one and reading to the end works great; for others, they like to take it in chronological order, or read it like a novel. I sincerely do not believe there is a "right way" or "wrong way" to study the Bible. That said, I do believe that the study of God's Word is not a sprint, but a marathon that lasts a lifetime: You need a plan.

I was raised on the King James Version (KJV). I grew up reading several passages in Sunday school, Bible quiz teams, and confirmation. My oldest brother gave me a Pilgrim Study Bible (KJV) around the time of my confirmation, and I still carry it today. I'd **STRONGLY** recommend getting a solid study Bible, and a good Bible commentary, and dictionary. These tools greatly help with understanding; offering personal views by the author(s) and cross references to other scripture for word definitions, cultural distinctions, context, and clarity.

I'll admit, as a youth, my interest in the Bible was all church driven, and my parents and pastor were great to talk to if I had any questions. Eventually, I decided that I wanted to read the Bible cover to cover. My pastor told me to start at the book of John, because the New Testament is directed more toward the church, which is what we are.

Now, starting at the book of John, that seemed like I was reading chapter 4 without reading chapters 1-3, right? However, the second piece of advice made sense. Start with the New Testament to try to understand the development and direction given to the church - which we are today. That said, I opened Matthew 1:1, and continued on through Revelation.

I'll admit, I honestly didn't 'take it all in' going through it that first time, but I got a high level understanding. So, then I went back to Genesis 1:1, read through Malachi, then re-read the New Testament again. This time it made more sense. I could recall some of the references to the Old Testament, which was very cool. In addition, reading the New Testament a second time, I caught things that I had missed, or didn't understand the first time.

In all honesty, that still happens each time I sit down with my Bible, even today. I fully believe God increases your understanding as you continue to study His Word. This is why I can confirm, from my own experience, that the Bible is God's *LIVING* Word! Hallelujah!

When I re-read Revelation, I developed a huge interest in the End Times (I played roll-playing games as a kid, so reading of dragons, demons, angels, and floating cities was pretty cool...). But, what did it mean to me and my life today, and into eternity?

Life Today: Dispensations and Prophecy

Remember how I said prophecy fulfillment builds credibility? Well, considering 2,000 prophecies have been fulfilled (in great detail) gives me great confidence in the credibility of the prophesies of the Bible. They started way back in Genesis, and continue all the way through Revelation. Fulfilled prophecies have helped to identify events to come, even the return of the Messiah Himself, Jesus Christ!

So, what about the way God interacts with Man in the Garden of Eden, the Old Testament, the New Testament, today, and even in the End Times? It seems there are different 'rules of engagement', right? I mean, Jesus wasn't even born at the time of the Old Testament, so people couldn't believe in Him at that time, right? It's a question I struggled with; until I was introduced to dispensationalism.

"A dispensation is a period of time during which man is tested in respect of obedience to some revelation of the will of God." - Scofield Reference Bible

Charles Caldwell Ryrie wrote an excellent book entitled *Dispensationalism Today.* He walks through the origins of dispensationalism and the differing views on how the times are segregated by theologians. This count can go from six to eight dispensations, depending on the writer. That said, there are seven general divisions:

1. Innocence - Initial creation
2. Conscience - Man is conscience of sin (Adam's fall)
3. Patriarchs - Noah through Abraham
4. Mossaic - Laws, Priesthood, Kings
5. Christian/Grace - Christ is born, church is born
6. Millennium - 1,000 year reign of Jesus on Earth
7. Eternity - Sin, death, evil destroyed - Heaven

1. God's interaction in each of these differs slightly but, the interaction back to God from man also differs. Let's look at "Innocence." God was alone until he created human beings. There was no sin, and God would walk with them in the Garden (Genesis 3:8). Some believe that this was actually Jesus in the garden since no man has ever seen the face of God (Exodus 33:20, John 1:18). I believe this is a position of faith for babies in the womb, newborns, or people with severe mental disabilities: they cannot understand, and therefore cannot make a choice to accept God's gift of Salvation. I refer to them as "innocent in Christ."

2. Eve is then persuaded by Satan to eat the forbidden fruit, which she does (Genesis 3:6). Then she passes it to Adam, who understands that the fruit is forbidden by God. Adam sees that Eve does not die, willingly eats the fruit, and God makes them conscious of their nakedness (sin - Genesis 3:7). They tried to hide, then tried to point the finger for their individual actions at someone else (Genesis

3:11-13). When sin entered the world, God cursed Satan, as well as His Creation (Genesis 3:14-21). I feel that this is the age of accountability (conscience) in human life: We understand we need to make a choice to follow Christ or not, whether at a young age or later in life.

3. Adam and Eve have children, and they go on to populate the earth. We then travel through the well known stories of the Old Testament, in which patriarchy is established. Noah and the flood - literally a cleansing of how horrible man had become (in such short time) - and on to Abraham and his families (Genesis 9 - 50). God was once again directly interacting with the lead patriarch of the family. This relates to our walk as youth in life, stepping out into the world as young adults.

4. Moses was where this shifted to establishing law, order, leadership, and governance among the great people (Exodus). God was now working through chosen people instead of just a patriarch. Moses and Aaron were His vessels, but we also see Miriam start to lead (worship).

"I want to make one note here: I believe the Bible is very clear that a woman is not to preach to congregations or teach adult education as these would conflict with the Bible's teaching on authority in the church (1 Timothy 2:12). However, I do believe this is the only limitation, and that women should be free to lead worship (as Miriam did - Exodus 15:20), and teach other women and children in the church body."

From here, there are several changes in leadership, laws, and government established (Joshua - Proverbs). Much of this was driven by people demanding changes; desiring judges and kings like other nations. This was not what God wanted, but he allowed it because of the people's desire (1 Samuel 8). Through all of this, God was still working through His prophets, which we see through the remaining books of the Old Testament (Ecclesiastes - Malachi). As we mature, we gain understanding of the rules of society, and we focus more on obedience for our lives.

5. Jesus is born (Matthew 1:17-25). This is the culmination of many prophecies, and many more are fulfilled during His 33 years of human life. Jesus is the Messiah, but not recognized by many Jewish leaders; therefore, they stuck to the law rather than accepting grace through Christ. This is the transition from law to grace, and is the focus of Paul's writing in the book of Romans.

The church is established, and this IS the dispensation that we live in today. The events that have taken place through the history of the world have fulfilled the final prophecies needed before He returns again to 'catch up' the church (1 Thessalonians 4:17), known as the Rapture. This is the next event to happen. Then, the world that is left behind (non-Believers in Jesus Christ), will enter into the Tribulation period (Revelation 4:1-19:11).

The Tribulation will be a time in which Satan will become the leader of the world (the Beast a.k.a. Antichrist). The third Temple will be built, and the Beast will allow temple worship the first 3.5 years, which will appear as 'peace' on earth. Then, the second Beast (a.k.a. the False Prophet) will demand all must worship the first Beast (Revelation 13:12). This ushers in last 3.5 years, in which anarchy, power, and greed will rule the day.

The selfish non-Believers will feel like they now have the freedom to do as they desire, and rebel against God's religious rules and authority. Those that defy the worship of the Beast, but turn to God, will be martyred (killed for their faith in God - Revelation 6:11). To the ungodly, this is victory; but to the Believer, this is 'Hell' on earth, until Jesus returns to end this time.

This represents our lives today. Jesus has manifested Himself to the world, and we see Him manifest into reality in several ways within our lives. Today, we have means to study and understand our relationship with Jesus as our Lord and Savior, and determine if we will be Raptured as Believers, or choose to face the judgement of God.

6. Jesus the Messiah King, the Lord of Lords, comes in the clouds with His army (Revelation 19:11-16). The first Beast and his worldly armies will gather to make war against them, but will be defeated. The first Beast and second Beast are then thrown into the Lake of Fire for eternity (Revelation 19:20), and Satan is chained in the bottomless pit (Revelation 20:1-3).

Jesus then sets up His Kingdom on earth which will reign for 1,000 years (Revelation 20). This is why this is called the Millennium (which means 1,000 years), or Millennial Kingdom (led from the cleansed third Temple). Temple sacrifices will resume, but will not include the sin offering, for that is addressed through Jesus's sacrifice on the Cross of Calvary for all men (Hebrews 9:12). God will be directly involved with His people to fulfill the remaining blessing to Israel.

There is still free will at this time, and there are those that will defy the Lord Jesus as King. At the end of the 1,000 years, Satan will be released from the bottomless pit for a short time, and he will deceive many nations (Revelation 20:8).

He will gather his army, which will number like the sand of the sea to fight against Jesus and His army at Jerusalem. Fire will then come down from Heaven and destroy the entire army at once (Revelation 20:9). Satan will then be cast into the Lake of Fire with the other two Beasts (Revelation 20:10).

Then all of the dead non-Believers will face judgement at the Great White Throne, and be cast into the Lake of Fire as well (Revelation 20:11-15).

I relate to this as cleaning up loose ends in our lives - unfinished business if you will. Every life has great moments to look back on and appreciate, as well as moments of regret - relationships and actions that we could cheer on, or that we need to correct with humility and forgiveness. I believe this inspires many of life's celebrations; as well as instigates deathbed confessions.

7. God then destroys the old Heaven and Earth (Revelation 21:1), creating a new Heaven and new Earth. New Jerusalem descends from the clouds, and becomes the dwelling place for Jesus and His Believers for all eternity. There is no time, no more sin, no more tears; only peace and love, and the light of Jesus Christ shines forever. Eternity (Revelation 21-22).

Life Today: The world we now live in

Pretty cool, right? So, that brings us up to today, the world we live in now. Going back to Matthew 24, Jesus states what signs we should be looking for in our world that help us understand when the End Times are nearing. A summary is offered in Matthew 24:3-14, and then more detail is given as the chapter continues.

Jesus's first warning is to be careful that you are not deceived (Matthew 24:4). How many times have we seen people follow another person that claims to have received a message from God, or that even claims to be God or Jesus Christ in the flesh? Cults are famous for this, especially over the last 50-70 years, and we were warned (Matthew 24:5). Rumors of wars, and nation battling against nation, famines and pestilence (Matthew 24:6-8).

These are common around the globe, and yet Jesus states that this is just the beginning of the sorrows to come. How often have you heard that there is so much hate in the world, and persecution building for the Christian church?

Persecution will continue through the Tribulation. There will be offense, betrayal, hate, lawlessness, and many false prophets that will deceive the nations (Matthew 24:9-12). Love will grow cold through that time, but those that remain faithful will be saved (Matthew 24:13). Through the Millennium, the Gospel will be preached, and then the end will come (Matthew 24:14).

As we walk through the chronology (timeline) of the End Times, we will get into much more detail about each of the events. But as we do, I want you to take into consideration the things that line up with what we are seeing in today's world.

Do you recognize the persecution of the Christian church today? Can you see the rise of religions that oppose Christianity, and global acceptance of them? Do you see religious leadership that is teaching a false message, denying the deity of Christ, and offering alternative ways to Salvation? Can you see a one world government, one world currency, and one world religion being promoted? Do you see worldly priorities on materialistic things, status and recognition, and thirst for power? Can you recognize the hate, arrogance, selfish greed, and self victimization for personal gain?

Do you see it? This is the world that we now live in. God knows human nature, and He realizes the effect that sin has in our lives. He has foretold this all through scripture, offering examples of failures when we turn from Him, and His grace when we simply accept Him for who He is. Jesus summarized our situation in just a few verses; isn't it amazing how spot on accurate His prophecy was?

People argue that some biblical prophecies were generic, and I agree. The real question should be, were they wrong? That answer is a resounding *NO!* A person taking an honest look at the reality of today's world can see the prophecies coming to life (more on 2020 living in Chapter 9). So, as we proceed on this journey, I want to reiterate that you actively read the Bible as your foundation for reality; the solid rock to stand on for truth...objective truth vs. subjective truth...

Read the papers, reports, social postings, and seek the truth behind those stories and situations. When you understand the truth of our world today, you will understand just how spot on God's Word explains humanity. The message to the churches in Revelation 2-3 still hold true, and cause so many of the situations we face today as Christ's church.

Take a moment to pray for wisdom as you continue to read His Word and open your heart to Him in prayer. Then let's move on to the next chapter...

Chapter 3
The Rapture... The next event?

Now that we've established where we are, we need to understand where we are going. This chapter will talk through the event called the Rapture. I personally believe this is the next event in God's timeline; however, there are others that think it will occur later in the Tribulation period and I want to take a fair approach to share those theories as well.

Won't that just add confusion? I hope not; instead, I hope it will promote you to research theories you develop from reading the Bible (or anything). It is very important that you create a strong foundation for the reason you believe what you believe, because at some point, you will most likely be challenged.

It is very important that you create a strong foundation for the reason you believe what you believe, because at some point, you will most likely be challenged.

Did you know that the word 'rapture' never appears in the Holy Bible? It's from the Latin translation 'rapere' of the Greek work 'harpzo'; to 'snatch' or 'catch up'. As a matter of fact, if we look up the word 'rapture' in my favorite dictionary (Websters 1828 version), it is defined as:

1. A seizing by violence.
2. Transport, ecstasy, violence of a pleasing passion, extreme joy or pleasure.
3. Rapidity of violence; a hurting along with velocity; as rolling with torrent rapture.
4. Enthusiasm; uncommon heat of imagination.

Um... that's not exactly what comes to mind when I think of the word 'rapture'. Is that what you thought the word meant? In today's dictionary, it maintains the above definitions, but also contains the Biblical event:

Theology. The experience, anticipated by some fundamental Christians, of meeting Christ midway in the air upon His return to earth.

YES! That's the one that makes sense to me, and the only way I've honestly heard the word used that I can remember. So, let's break that down a bit to ensure we have a solid understanding of this meaning, and how the world views this...

The first half of that definition is 'The experience, anticipated by some fundamental Christians...'. This is actually a great definition when we break down the verbiage used. 'The experience' basically means an event that will be experienced, and 'anticipated' means this event will occur in the future. Then we hit a key word, 'fundamental'. When we look up that word, it is defined as 'being an essential part of, a foundation of something'. How true this is.

When Jesus Christ was resurrected, and ascended to Heaven (Luke 24), He became the first person to do so (John 3:13). He ascended to prepare a place, and then He will come and take us (John 14:3), which is referring to the event of the Rapture. This is essential for two reasons.

The fact that Jesus was resurrected is a key foundation of the Christian faith. Paul states this very boldly in 1 Corinthians 15:14, 17:

'If Christ has not been raised, then our preaching is vain, and your faith is also vain...And if Christ has not been raised, your faith is worthless; you are still in your sins.'

Jesus stating that He is going to prepare a place for us, and that He will come back to take us, should create an incredible hope for the Believer. He's preparing a place for us, and then will come back to take us, and bring us to that place He is preparing for us! How awesome is that?!

The second part of the definition, the actual rapture event, is actually referred to as the "Believer's Hope" in some Bibles. This is an event that will only save the innocent in Christ, and Believers; the rest will be left behind. Paul describes the event, in chronological order, as it will occur on earth (1 Thessalonians 4:13-18).

So the definition is pretty spot on. Now, let's consider the effect of that event. All Believers, and innocent in Christ are taken from the earth. Who does that leave behind? Those that have chosen not to accept Jesus Christ as their Lord and Savior. People are going to disappear instantly, in the twinkling of an eye (1 Corinthians 15:51-58), with no explanation for non-Believers.

I will also add that I, personally, believe the Holy Spirit is removed at that point as well. This makes way for the Antichrist to have his way on earth unrestrained (2 Thessalonians 2:5-7). In addition, I believe John sees the 'Perfect Spirit' (Seven Spirits) in Heaven when he is shown the rapture event (Revelation 4:1).

Imagine the horror that will be felt by those left behind. Non-Believing parents seeing innocent children disappear, and two close friends sitting together, or working together, and the unsaved see the saved disappear. To the unsaved, there will be no rhyme or reason for this event. I would imagine the media, and worldly science will play it up as aliens, or some other phenomenon. They will feel loss, resentment, fear, hate, anger, and chaos will reign from people acting on those emotions. The rapture will definitely be a world changing event.

*The rapture will definitely be
a world changing event.*

We've talked about what will happen, so now let's focus on when it will occur. There are three main theories as to when this happens: Pre-Tribulation, Mid-Tribulation, and Post-Tribulation. Let's review each of these theories and hopefully help understand the basis for each of them.

Pre-Tribulation Rapture theory

This is the most common theory among Biblical Scholars, and is my own personal belief as well. Pre-Tribulation means the rapture event occurs before the Tribulation begins. The main theme here, is that the church would be pulled out of the world, so they would not experience the events of the rapture. What does scripture say?

As I stated previously, the disciple John was transported through a door that was opened to Heaven (Revelation 4:1). This is believed to be the rapture, and the door is suppose to represent Jesus (as the way to Heaven). John enters and describes what he sees in Heaven, and I believe this is what Believers will experience as we enter Heaven as well.

The church (Believers) is mentioned in detail through chapters two and three of Revelation. In fact, Revelation 3:10 seems to state the church will be removed, so that He can pour out His wrath on those who chose not to accept Jesus as Lord and Savior. This is the entire population that will remain on the earth:

'Because thou has kept the word of my patience, I also will keep thee from the hour of temptation, which shall come upon all the world, to try them that dwell on the earth.'

Also, after Revelation 4:1, they are not mentioned as being on earth again. Technically, the word 'churches' is not mentioned again until Revelation 22:16; but, the new Jerusalem (eternal dwelling for the church) is discussed in Revelation 21. Some believe they come back with Jesus in 19:11, but we'll discuss that later in the book. The point is, the church doesn't appear to remain on the earth for the seven years of the Tribulation.

Revelation 14 and 16 both speak of God's wrath being poured out on to humanity during the Tribulation. Romans 5:9 says that since Jesus justified us through His sacrifice for our sin on the Cross of Calvary, that we shall be saved from wrath through Him. Some people believe this is referring to eternal judgement; however, as a literal translator, the same words and meanings are used within these verses. From a literal standpoint of Paul's message in Romans, this seems to make perfect sense.

It follows the theory of Dispensationalism, and the distinction between Israel and the church. The basis of salvation is always the same, grace through faith (Ephesians 2:8); however, God's prophecies are distinct for Israel and the church. The prophecy for Israel of 70 weeks in Daniel 9:24-27 is said to have a parenthesis between week 69 and week 70 (which is the current dispensation). Then, the rapture, and the 70th week will proceed, which is the Tribulation. That is the preparation of Israel (and the world) for His return to setup His Kingdom (Deuteronomy 4:29-30; Jeremiah 30; Ezekiel 22:18-22).

Heaven shows the church; but, also includes those that have been martyred for their faith in the Word of God, and testimony during the Tribulation. This is shown as the Lamb (Jesus) opens the fifth Seal; they are in white robes, under the alter (Revelation 6:9-11). This shows that they will live their lives as Christians, and that their faith brings them immediately to Heaven when they die.

There are 24 elders pictured, which is a full representation of the entire church (Revelation 4:1-5:14). We'll review alternate views on this later; but for now, you can compare this to when King David's entire priesthood was represented in the Old Testament (1 Chronicles 24:7-18), a number dictated by God (1 Chronicles 24:19).

Mid-Tribulation Rapture theory

The mid-Tribulation theory is the least accepted theory in theological circles. The evidence within scripture is based on assumption more than actual statements. All of that said, I want to be fair, and offer some education as to where the theory stems from. I don't want to state that it is not possible; because my understanding is limited vs. God's understanding (Isaiah 55:8).

It is agreed that there is a major event that happens half way through the Tribulation period of seven years (Daniel 7:25, 9:27, 12:7-11; Revelation 12:6, 14, 13:5). This is argued to be the sign that Jesus is referring to as he takes His disciples through the Olivet Discourse (Matthew 29-31, Mark 13:14-23).

Revelation chapters 5-9 shows Jesus breaking the seals of the scroll, and suffering and difficulties for Believers as well as non-Believers. The theory is, this is not the wrath of God; instead, the true wrath of God is the second half of the Tribulation. Those that adhere to this view, then also point to Romans 5:9 to show the church will be pulled out before the wrath of God falls on the earth (Revelation 14-17-18:24).

Some theorists state that Revelation 11:15, the sounding of the seventh trumpet, ushers in His return. Then, in Revelation 11:17, then elders refer to Him as 'He was, and is" suggesting that He has already come... so this is stating Jesus is returning after the Tribulation starts, but before Revelation 11:17.

Overall, the theory is that Christians also have disobeyed God, and should experience the first part of the Tribulation (first 3.5 years), but not the finality of God's wrath (last 3.5 years). They agree this is the best reasoning for Scriptural emphasis to divide the Tribulation into two parts.

Post-Tribulation Rapture theory

The main point of this theory is that the church will remain on earth through the entire Tribulation period. Believers would be raised up at the end of the seven year period, right before Armageddon (in some theories). Then, Believers would return with Jesus when He comes back to earth to setup His Millennial Kingdom.

Some of the biggest Scriptural arguments for this theory is found in Matthew 24:29-31, 1 Thessalonians 4:15-17, and finally Revelation 20:4-6. There are others, but these are the ones that are pointed to most often in my own discussions with others.

This view has become more popular lately, especially in Evangelical circles, due to the apparent decline in Christian faith, doctrine, and morals within the church and its leaders. People that agree with this theory, also believe scripture teaches the resurrection of the church will occur at the visible coming of Jesus in the clouds. This theory falls more in line with Revelation 19:11.

To summarize, Post-Tribulation theorists believe the Rapture is not a separate event; but that it is part of the second coming of Christ at the end of the Tribulation. I will also admit that Revelation 4:5 was the verse that kept me digging into the Post-Tribulation theory. It sounded like the first resurrection was a one-time event (the Rapture). I feel it is clear that scripture says it ends here, but does not say it starts here.

My opinion? I believe the events appear unique: We meet Him in the clouds for the Rapture; He descends from the clouds in the second coming. The church is absent from Revelations 4-19, which is the seven years of Tribulation. I believe this validates the Pre-Tribulation theory. Be ready!

Are Old Testament Saints resurrected/raptured?

One other piece to consider is the Old Testament saints (Believers / Faithful to God). There are some that believe the opening of the tombs at the time of Jesus's death (Matthew 27:52) was showing the resurrection of these saints. This would also fall in line with the thinking that the twenty four elders (Revelation 4:4) would be twelve from the Old Testament (tribes) and twelve from the New Testament (apostles).

I personally believe the Old Testament saints will be resurrected at the time of the Millennium, which I will explain further once we get there; therefore, I don't believe they are in Heaven at this time, but their eternal souls are in the safety of 'Paradise' (Abraham's Bosom - Luke 16:22, 23:43). They are in the hand of God the Father, and no one has the power to snatch them out (John 10:29).

Regarding the 24 elders in Heaven, I believe that is a representation of the church. Notice we only see them bowing down to worship the Lamb, Jesus. That would not represent worship as directed in the Old Testament to the saints.

Are Tribulation martyrs resurrected/raptured?

What about Christians that die for their faith in the Tribulation (martyrs)? We only see the souls of those martyrs in Heaven (Revelation 6:9-11) vs. resurrected bodies in Heaven. Then, at the end of the Tribulation, they are raised as the final piece of the first resurrection (Revelation 20:5), and they reign with Jesus in the Millennium. We'll lay that out a little better when we get there...

Chapter 4
The first half - Tribulation

Whether you believe the Rapture is the next event or not, the events continue to move forward. The events will ping pong a little bit from what is happening in Heaven, and what is experienced on earth. Note that some events in Heaven trigger events on earth, and others do not. I have created a timeline through the book of Revelation which maps out the events, including where they occur, which I have included as a reference if you'd like to use that for tracking this journey.

I'll use Revelation as our main roadmap; as needed, I will reference other scripture to paint the complete picture...

On earth, we have a continuation of the events that we see in the world today (Matthew 24:8). Natural catastrophes increase in frequency, and a strong movement toward dependance on man's wisdom, technology, and power through bullying and self-righteous agendas that promote anarchy. Tensions continue to mount as there are smaller local (turf) wars, and threats of greater wars. Christianity and the Bible are portrayed to promote hate and cause further division. This draws people's faith away from God, in their desperation to seek relief and harmony elsewhere (2 Timothy 3). This creates an opportunity to push world leadership, and the Antichrist to be welcomed.

When John enters Heaven (Revelation 4:1-11), he sees God the Father's Throne Room. John describes this in detail, giving us a beautiful picture of how awesome this place is. The scene then shows God the Father on the Throne holding a scroll (Revelation 5:1), and points out that no one in Heaven or Earth is worthy to open the scroll. Then Jesus (the sacrificed Lamb - Revelation 5:6) steps forward, and takes the scroll from the Father's hand (Revelation 5:7), for He alone is worthy to open it. All of Heaven rejoices, and shouts praise to the Lamb (Jesus).

Jesus breaks open the first seal.

Enter, the Beast (Antichrist, first horseman (white) - Revelation 6:1). On earth, a man will step forward; respected for his great ability to speak, to remain calm and collected, and lead people (Revelation 13:5). I believe he will be attractive, humble in appearance, but influential as he was in the Garden of Eden (Genesis 3).

As the Antichrist conquers the nations of the earth with strength, he will grow in his pride (2 Thessalonians 2:4). He is not of Jewish descent (Revelation 13:1-10); but, he will restore worship for the Jewish people in their rebuilt third temple.

It is believed the two witnesses (Revelation 11) start to preach at this time. The Beast allows this temple worship in an attempt to denounce Christianity by promoting works through Orthodox worship vs. grace through Jesus Christ.

He will forge a peace treaty with Israel for seven years (Daniel 9:27), while growing in leadership status among the United Nations. The Beast will appear as a peacemaker for the world. This will create a false hope, which is truly a great deception by the Beast, to gain loyalty from the people (more in Revelation 13).

Jesus breaks open the 2nd, 3rd and 4th seals

The 2nd (red-war), 3rd (black-famine) and 4th (pale-death) horsemen are released on the earth (Revelation 6:3-8). Hatred, selfishness, vanity, materialism, and defiance will be society's anthem, forcing actions that will lead to further violence. Individual desires and privileged attitudes will take priority; accountability toward others will dwindle with everyone pointing the finger of blame at each other (2 Timothy 3:1-9).

The shortage of workers and lack of production of even basic items will create a demand for goods, with no supply being available. Basic utilities will fail to be maintained, which will produce outages, droughts, famines, and eventually a great death toll (Luke 21:11, Matthew 24:6-8). This will promote more fear, desperation, and a survival of the fittest mentality.

Jesus breaks open the fifth seal

We then turn back to Heaven to see the souls of martyrs for Christ, killed during the Tribulation, wearing white robes before the throne of God (Revelation 6:9). They cry out desiring God's justice to be poured out onto the world that has chosen not to accept Him. The martyrs are instructed to rest, until the other Believers that will be killed for their faith during the Tribulation join them (Revelation 6:11). It will happen soon...

Jesus breaks open the sixth seal

The people on earth are filled with shock and horror, as supernatural events have global impacts. A great earthquake, perhaps many of them, will most likely shift land (tectonic plates) and provoke the eruption of one or more super-volcanoes. This would spew massive amounts of smoke, ash, and lava into the air, blackening out the sun and discoloring the sky and moon (Revelation 6:12-14). The non-Believing world will explain this as natural phenomenon, the excessive effects of climate change, or some other reasoning that is consistent with their theories.

However, there will be some that understand the times, and He (Jesus) who is coming. They understand their selfish ways, desires of the world, and most important their denial of Jesus Christ through their lives. Like the demons that understand their fate (James 2:19), they too will shudder. Their fear will drive them to try to hide in the rocks, or mountains (Revelation 6:15), begging for the rocks to crush them. They foolishly believe death would deliver them from the wrath of God, and the justice they deserve for their denial of His Son, Jesus Christ, as Lord and Savior (Revelation 6:16).

During this time (Revelation 7:1-8), an Angel of the Lord places a seal on the forehead of 144,000 undefiled Jews (Revelation 14:1-5) ; 12,000 from each of the twelve tribes of Judah. They will preach the Gospel message across the earth, and none of them die during the Tribulation (see Revelation 14:1). This will be reverting back to how God spread His message to Israel in the Old Testament: The 144,000 and the two witnesses are the prophets of the Tribulation period; preaching the Gospel to the entire world (Matthew 24:14)!

History shows Jesus, the Son of God, has been born, died, and lives again today. Their message will be the Gospel message of Jesus Christ; showing Him to be their Lord and Savior, as well as their Messiah King! Old Testament prophecy and teaching are today's reality...Hallelujah!

The next section (Revelation 7:9-17) seems to be a parenthesis; perhaps a glimpse into the future or maybe to show the results of the 144,000's efforts. John sees a vision showing a multitude of people, with white robes, and palm branches in their hands. It is important to point out that scripture states they are from all nations, kindreds (races), tongues (languages), standing together before the Throne of Jesus, praising Him (Revelation 7:9). God does not show favoritism, racism, or preference based on anything but the intentions of the heart of the individual (Romans 2:11, Hebrews 4:12).

John states that the number of them is uncountable, but an elder tells him that these are the people that accept Jesus as Lord and Savior during the Great Tribulation (Revelation 7:14 - the last 3.5 years). Some believe the number of people saved at this time will be greater than the number saved through the history of mankind. WOW!

Imagine that challenge. The Holy Spirit has been removed at the Rapture, so you are now without 'God-conscience'. If you deny the Beast; accepting Jesus as your personal Lord and Savior, you will be killed (Revelation 13:15). This reality, is a great declaration to the benefit of accepting Jesus as Lord and Savior today, while we have the freedom to do so! Please consider that truth today!

Jesus breaks open the seventh seal

In Heaven, seven angels are given seven trumpets (Revelation 8:1), and the prayers of saints are given to another angel in a censor (bowl) to offer on the Golden Alter before the Throne of God. When these were burned, the smell was savory to God. The angel then used the censor to take some of the fire, and tossed that fire back onto the earth (Revelation 8:5); symbolizing God's wrath to come. The seven angels then readied to sound their respective trumpets.

1st, 2nd, 3rd, and 4th trumpets (the one thirds)

On earth (Revelation 8:7-9), people are frightened by thundering lightning storms, earthquakes, and what appears to be voices from the heavens. This fear turns to terror as hail, fire and blood rained down on the earth. One third of the trees and all of the green grass around the world is burned up.

A great asteroid, a mountain of mass, falls from the sky into the sea (salt water). The impact is so great, that it destroys one third of the ships that are in the seas. One third of the sea turns to blood, which kills one third of all sea creatures.

Another burning mass (like a great star) falls from the sky (Revelation 8:12) and lands on one third of the rivers and natural fountains (fresh water) around the globe. One third of the water will become bitter, like 'wormwood'; therefore, they will name that burning star 'Wormwood'. Many people will die because the waters will become undrinkable.

Then there will be changes in the heavenly bodies. One third of the sun will appear to be darkened, and its light will not shine for nearly one third of the days going forward. One third of the moon and stars will no longer be seen; as if they were darkened or removed. Their light will be gone for nearly one third of each night as well.

John then sees an angel flying through the upper skies of earth, shouting a warning to those that remain on the earth. "Woe, woe, woe to all inhibitors of the earth; for there are still three trumpets that the angels will sound" (Revelation 8:13). This was a warning to those on the earth, stating what has been seen were results from the first four angels sounding their trumpets. Each of the remaining three trumpets will be a 'woe' or further suffering as God continues to pour His wrath on mankind.

As we continue through the woes on the earth, we will read descriptions of creatures that are allegories vs. actual creatures that will be present on the earth. There are theories as to what each component or beast may represent; however, that is all speculation. We do not have the full understanding of God; therefore, some mysteries will never be known in our lifetimes (Ecclesiastes 8:17).

The results of the events are what are important; that is what will be experienced by the people on earth at this time.

Fifth trumpet (plagues)

An angel is sent to the earth (Revelation 9:1, Isaiah 14:12), which appeared as a falling star, and then the angel was given a key to the bottomless pit. As the earth opens, smoke pours out, which darkens the air and blocks out the sunlight (Revelation 9:2). There will be great persecution against the 144,000 that are spreading the Gospel message (Revelation 9:4).

This will most likely be a focused effort to serve as an example, and warning to other Christians. They will experience intense physical pain, possibly as Jesus did with scourging and whips, that will feel like scorpion stings. This will be public torture, fear will cause mankind to desire death, but they will be kept alive (Revelation 9:6).

Those inflicting the torture are men (Revelation 9:7) who are in leadership roles (gold crowns). Most likely, these men will have dedicated their loyalty to the Beast, or be controlled by demons (which some think may be the creatures described). They are led by the angel of the bottomless pit (Apollyon/Abaddon), and are filled with the Spirit of Antichrist (Revelation 9:11). Many believe the details used by John were the only way he could describe the heavy war vehicles, weapons, and flying machines seen by humans throughout this event. This is the first woe on the earth, and there are two more to come...

Sixth Trumpet (200,000,000 man army)

The four angels are set loose from the Euphrates rivers (Revelation 9:14), at this time that was appointed by God. Most likely, these are again demons that possess the leader(s) of the 200,000,000 person army (Revelation 9:16). Once again, John's descriptions most likely are best efforts to describe the war machines of that day. The results of this army; one third of all humans are killed. Note there is no distinction as to whom is killed, but simply one third of all mankind (Revelation 9:18). They do not care who they trample for their agenda.

The survivors of these actions see these events, but do not turn their hearts to Jesus (Revelation 9:20-21). They specifically will not give up the works of their hands (pride of accomplishments), their worship of devils (Satan worship), their worship of idols made from any materials. In addition, they did not repent of murders, sorcery, sexual desires outside of what God has dictated (one man and one woman who are married), or their thefts (most likely a wide variety of examples).

How is this viewed as Believers?

In Revelation chapter 10, I believe that God creates a break in the action. This allows John (and us) to digest what has been shared, and consider how these events should be viewed as Believers. The vision is heard by John alone; notice he is told not to record what he hears initially. This is not an event that will be seen on earth.

There has been so much destruction, so much damage to Creation, so many deaths. Is it disturbing that this has been allowed by God? Is this what Justice from a loving God looks like? These are very real concerns, and can present emotional challenges to Believers.

The little book, only mentioned here, (Revelation 10:2) is a book of events that are being played out. Notice, John eats the book (ingesting it). It is sweet in his mouth (initial impression), but then bitter in his belly (gut feeling). The events here should cause joy as well as bitterness... Why?

As we take in the events, we feel like the martyrs in Revelation 7, right? It's about time we see some of God's justice! Father, let your judgement fall on those that do not accept your free gift of Grace through Jesus Christ your Son! That attitude, is the same one that Jonah held (Jonah 4).

Then, there is a realization that the events are affecting all people, not just the wicked. Christians, as well as the 144,000 sealed Jewish evangelists, are under intense torture. And not only that, but there is a realization that non-Believers (maybe even some close to us, loved ones) will face God's wrath, and will be tossed to the Lake of Fire that burns for all eternity. This is gut-wrenching, and creates a bitter feeling in our stomach (Revelation 10:10).

When we are in heaven, there is nothing more we can do but desire the Day of the Lord (Isaiah 2:12, 2 Corinthians 1:14)! But while we are on earth, we need to remember our call from Jesus, the great commission (Mark 16:15). God does not desire that even one should be lost, and neither should we (2 Peter 3:9). This should drive Christians to reach out in love and hope with the Gospel message to as many as we can while we are alive! Go and share today!

A moment to reflect

The most common questions that have come from my own discussions about the End Times are these: Why doesn't God just deal with Satan, and those that are denying Him as Lord and Savior; then move forward to eternal peace for Believers in Heaven? Why does there have to be suffering through the Tribulation for good people as well? Good questions, so let's see if scripture addresses this topic...

How many people do you think God wants to see go to Hell and ultimately the Lake of Fire forever? The answer is none. Peter states that God does not wish that anyone would perish, but all would repent (2 Peter 3:9). Think back to Revelation 7: The number of people that are saved during the Tribulation is likely greater than those saved throughout all human history. What draws them to the Lord to become Believers? Did the events allowed to take place influence their decisions? I think so... Fear can be a great motivator, especially when it becomes reality.

The number of people that are saved during the Tribulation is likely greater than those saved throughout all human history.

The opposite side of that coin is the alternate result. It's possible that those that turned to Christ during the Tribulation would not have, if these events would not have occurred (2 Corinthians 1:6-11). So, is the end result worth it? If we believe that we deserve free will, then it *IS* worth it (Romans 8:28). So, ingesting the reality of the events written in this little book is then 'bitter-sweet'.

The two witnesses

The first half of the Tribulation ends with God giving His power to two witnesses who will testify in Jerusalem (Revelation 11:3). Some speculate that this is Enoch and Elijah because they never suffered physical death (Hebrews 9:27). Others think one of the witnesses may be Moses because of the plagues he can control; but I believe Enoch fits scripture best (Hebrews 11:5), and God can give powers to whom He wills (1 Corinthians 12:11). Either way, they are given supernatural powers like in Old Testament times.

They will prophesy for 1,260 days, which is why we place their preaching at the time of the Antichrist's initial step into power. If anyone tried to hurt them, they will be destroyed by fire that comes from their mouth (Revelation 11:5). This is not figurative, as the next verse confirms they must be killed by that process. They have power to control rainfall, plagues, and can turn water to blood at their will (Revelation 11:6).

The angel (now referred to as a Beast) emerges from the bottomless pit to lead the events of the fifth trumpet. To be clear, this is not the same Beast as Antichrist; instead, this is an evil angel (demon) that is driven by the spirit of Antichrist. The agenda is the same, but there are unique players with respective roles to play.

He will eventually overpower and kill the two witnesses (Revelation 11:7), because their testimony has been a source of constant annoyance and hate for those who have chosen to follow the Beast (Antichrist). Leaders proclaim that their bodies should lie in the street, partly to humiliate them (custom), but to also announce that the world can celebrate the end of their preaching. This will occur at the sight that Jesus was crucified (Revelation 11:8-10).

One interesting point: John says that all nations will see their bodies and rejoice (Revelation 11:9). This was not possible without today's technology which can share info around the world on demand; once again fulfilling scripture to every detail. After 3.5 days God enters the two witnesses; they will stand back up, and then ascend to Heaven (Revelation 11:11-12). The world watches in shock and awe. A few fear God's power, yet remain unrepentant; instead, being full of wrath (Revelation 11:18).

The second woe, and seventh trumpet

On earth, after the two witnesses ascend, there is another great earthquake. One tenth of Jerusalem will fall down, and seven thousand people die. At that point, the remaining people in Jerusalem gave God glory out of their fear (Revelation 11:14). The second woe is done, and the third will happen quickly.

In Heaven, a great voice proclaims the kingdoms of earth are the Lord's, and He will reign forever (Revelation 11:15-19). The 24 elders sitting before God, fall on their faces and offer worship to God to celebrate the time of judgement that has come. The Temple of God (in Heaven) was opened, and the Ark of the Covenant is seen, followed by several natural disasters on the earth.

Call to reality

As we read through the first 3.5 years of the coming Tribulation, what thoughts are coming to your mind? What would you do if you were put in a position to deal with the events that are spoken of by John in the revelation that was given to him?

The view of this coming time is truly based on where your heart is. Why? Because many will feel the pressure that is spoken of here, they will bow to intimidation and fear, and they will give in to worshiping the Beast or be killed. That is reality.

The real question is where is your heart?

*The first half of the Tribulation is completed...
now on to the Great Tribulation...*

Chapter 5
The Great Tribulation - part 1

We have walked through the first half of the Tribulation. We covered the following situation on earth:

- Jesus broke the seven seals of the End Times Scroll
- The Antichrist's initial power and conquest
- The third Jewish Temple is built and sacrifices restored
- Natural disasters increase in intensity and frequency
- Two witnesses testified, killed, raised, and asceneded
- 144,000 Jews marked to spread the Gospel message
- Christianity faces its greatest persecution
- Seven trumpets have sounded, with events explained
- Believers' bittersweet feelings of the events

As we move to the second half of the Tribulation (a.k.a. the Great Tribulation), we will now see the Antichrist assume global power, and worship of him will be setup through a global false religion. God's wrath will continue to be poured out on the world, with more focus on Satan's work and devoted followers. This will culminate into the battle of Armageddon, and closing of the Tribulation Dispensation to enter Christ's Millennial Kingdom.

Satan and one third of angels cast down to earth

God recaps the history of the struggle between God, His people, and Lucifer/Satan in Revelation 12. The first woman represents the Wife of God - Israel (12 stars in crown). The woman's life (history of Israel) has been a story to bring forth the birth of the Son, Jesus. The dragon is Satan (also named the Devil), and he tries to devour the child (Jesus - trying to remove the effects of His life). The Son, Jesus, is born and then delivered to His place beside God the Father in Heaven. The finished work of Jesus Christ on the Cross of Calvary was the kill shot to Satan's head, as promised in the Garden of Eden (Genesis 3:15, Revelation 12:11).

The events starting in Revelation 12:7 are interesting to interpret. As I think of the conclusion of Genesis 3, Lucifer has already made his stand against God, and is damned for his actions. In Revelation 12:4 we see that when Satan is cast out of Heaven, he draws one third of the stars in Heaven (angels) with him. They are cast down to earth, but that is before the man-child is born in Revelation 5. So how does that timing work? Were Satan and the angels cast down to Heaven before Christ? Was that because of the actions in the Garden of Eden? I don't believe scripture supports that - here's why...

If we look back to the Old Testament book of Job, we see that sons of God (angels) ritually came to present themselves (check in) with God the Father. Why do I believe they are angels? Because no man has ascended to Heaven before Jesus (John 3:13). These 'sons of God' would be heavenly creatures, of which we hear of angels at that time. Therefore, it would appear that all angels, faithful or not, would be appearing before God in Heaven.

Another interesting point, Satan is not referred to as Lucifer. I believe this is because Lucifer had a level of great respect in Heaven (Ezekiel 28) before his arrogance grew and he believed he would ascend higher than God (Isaiah 14:12-17). Just as the old man dies as we become Believers, it would appear the old man dies when we choose to stand against God (this again promote free will for all of God's creation). I believe God only refers to Satan by his angelic name, Lucifer, the anointed Cherub (angel), when making the point as to what great heights and honor, in God's Kingdom, he has fallen from.

So, it is assumed that Satan and his angels still have access to Heaven even though they have chosen to rebel against God. This is even further confirmed in Revelation 12:7 in which Michael and the 'obedient' angels fight against Satan and 'disobedient' angels. Then we see Satan (Devil) and his disobedient angels cast down to the earth (Revelation 12:9). Following this, there is a celebration in Heaven; Satan and his angels are kicked out forever, and the warning to those on earth that seems to fit in well with the second half of the Tribulation (Great Tribulation):

"...the devil is come down to you, having great wrath, because he knows his time is short" - Revelation 12:12

There is one other thing that God does here, that fits so well with His character toward His people. God offers hope. The Devil is going to take out his wrath on the people of God that brought forward Jesus (Jews/Israel - Revelation 12:13). His efforts will fail, and God will deliver His wife (Israel) to safety (believed to be Petra - more on that later...) for the remainder of the Tribulation (Revelation 12:14). Then, He details the events of Heaven and Earth through the Great Tribulation to John. So let's walk through this...

Beast out of the Sea (Antichrist)

In Heaven, John sees the Beast rising out of the Sea (Revelation 13). The 'sea' is symbolic here, as it is referring to where this beast is emerging from. Most people interpret the sea to mean a non-Israel location. This would mean that the Beast (Antichrist) will rise up from a nation that is not Israel, but could be anywhere else.

NOTE: Many also believe that this person will most likely be of Arab descent based on the sharp differences between Isaac and Ishmael (Genesis 17). This also falls in line with the belief of many people; that Ishmael is the father to the Arab people.

On earth, we know the first horseman is the Antichrist (a.k.a. the Beast), and we saw him take his first steps into leadership with the breaking of the first seal (Revelation 6:2). The Beast will continue to grow in power, and become the leader of a 10-nation union that will govern the world (Revelation 13:1-2). This is why many believe there will be a one-world government through the Great Tribulation period (a.k.a. new Roman Empire).

It is believed that an attempt will be made on the Antichrist's life; people will even believe that he dies, then comes back to life again (Revelation 13:3). This will mimic Christ's own death and resurrection, making him seem more 'god-like'. The world will grow to worship the Beast, and will believe he is the ultimate leader, and unstoppable (Revelation 13:4).

The Beast is an excellent speaker, and will continue to promote himself, and make great promises to the world. He will grow in power and his ego will thrive on the authority that the world continues to give him. His message will be subtle, but eventually, he will speak out directly against God, the Tabernacle, and those that dwell in Heaven (Revelation 12:6).

Ultimately, he will agree to have an image of himself setup in the Tabernacle as foretold by Daniel (chapters 9, 11, 12). This 'Abomination of Desolation' will lead to the remaining Jews in Judea fleeing to safety in the mountains (Matthew 24:15-21). Also, he will encourage his followers to make war with any that claim faith in God, or follow Jesus (Revelation 12:7). And then a solemn warning:

"The names of all who worship the Beast, will not be found written in the Book of Life." - Revelation 12:8

Beast out of the Land (False Prophet)

In Heaven, John then saw a Beast come out of the land, which represents Israel (Palestine). He had two great horns, and spoke like a dragon (several interpretations). Let's focus on what he does with his power and authority...

On earth, this man will be in a position of authority from a religious standpoint, a False Prophet from Israel / Jewish descent. He will also be an excellent speaker, and a natural leader; to the point of gaining respect among people much like the first Beast. He will also have great powers, like the Old Testament prophets, and this will create great 'awe' among men (Revelation 13:13).

The False Prophet's primary purpose is to deceive the masses, and create a one world religion that does not worship or honor God. He will lead his followers, and many in the world to worship the first Beast (Revelation 13:12) as a Messiah-like figure. He will convince the masses to create an image as a testimony to the first Beast (Revelation 13:14), and to set it up in the Tabernacle to worship it...further mocking God.

Finally, the False Prophet (second Beast) has the power to bring the image of the first Beast to life, and it will speak great things. The one world religion will team with the one world government, requiring every person to give their allegiance to the Beast, or be put to death (Revelation 13:15). When they choose to accept the Beast, they will receive a permanent mark in their forehead or in their right hand (Revelation 13:16).

This 'mark' will have a global effect in everyone's lives. The Beast will declare this mark is required to buy or sell products (Revelation 13:17). The pressure to get the mark just to purchase bread or milk, or run your business, will be too much pressure for some. They will give in, and take the mark for personal gain, or to provide for their families. The mark is a human number, six hundred sixty-six (666) (Revelation 13:18). Many believe this will *not* be a straight forward tattoo or brand that says '666'; but, perhaps a bar code, inserted micro chip, or personal identifier of some type...

The point is, God's Word is clear about the warning, regardless of how sneaky the Devil tries to be. This will occur in some scenario. Those that worship the Beast, taking his mark, are choosing eternal damnation on themselves. Their name will not be in the Book of Life (Revelation 12:8), and those not in the Book of Life will be cast into the Lake of Fire (Revelation 20:15).

The announcements of the Gospel, and fate of nations

As the Antichrist (first Beast) and False Prophet (second Beast) come into power and develop great influence around the world, we see another set of events in Heaven...

An angel flies through the heavens with the Gospel message and a warning to worship God, the Creator of all things. This states that the Gospel message will be shared with every nation, kindred, tongue and people (Revelation 14:6-7). They are being warned to fear God, for His hour of judgement has arrived on all creation.

A second angel declares that Babylon is fallen! This may seem like a city; but it is referring to the False Prophet. Much like Israel was the 'wife' of God the Father, Babylon is a 'harlot' (prostitute), luring mankind into adultery against God. She has lured many away from God (Revelation 14:8), and her followers will join in the wrath she shall receive.

Then, a third angel announces once again that anyone that worships the Beast, or takes on his mark, will experience the wrath of God. They will be tormented with fire and brimstone in the presence of the holy angels. There is a theory that those who choose to worship the Beast will be tormented day and night forever in the Lake of Fire (Revelation 14:11) vs. those that simply do not accept Jesus, who may be consumed (removed from existence).

Rewards for good works, and coming judgements

The topic of grace vs. works is a strong point of contention within the Believers community; therefore, I want to share a few thoughts on this from scripture (specifically to the rewards for works). Revelation 14:13 is a confirmation that our works will follow us when we die. So, is this just the good works? Is it all rewards? No.

There are two judgements that will occur; one for Believers, one for non-Believers. The judgement for Believers is called the BEMA judgement (Romans 14:8-10; 1 Corinthians 3:10-15, 9:24-27; 2 Corinthians 5:10). This judgement is as a flame of fire (note the eyes of Jesus - Revelation 1:14), burning through the actions taken that were not God honoring (most likely honored ourselves), and reveals the precious stones.

The foundation is laid by Jesus. Our salvation (becoming Christians) is accomplished through our acceptance of His finished work; however, we remain accountable for our personal actions as Christians. This testing, is a judgement in which Jesus reviews what we did as Christians during our life.

Actions all start with intentions: Sometimes actions 'look' good to everyone else, but the intentions are purely selfish. Jesus sees through this in His judgement (Hebrews 4:12), for these selfish actions (intentions that are not glorifying to God) are burned away as the wood, hay, and straw. The God-glorifying actions (intentions) are the precious stones which we will be rewarded.

The important factor is that this judgement occurs in Heaven. And who get's to Heaven? Believers. And how does one become a Believer? Only by accepting Jesus Christ as our Lord and Savior, and handing our life over to Him and His will (John 3:16, 14:6). So to summarize - the BEMA judgement is Jesus reviewing the intentions of each Believer's actions.

"Each man must be careful how he builds on it. For no man can lay a foundation other than the one which is laid, which is Jesus Christ. Now if any may builds on the foundation gold, silver, previous stones, wood, hay, straw, each man's work will become evident; for the day will show it because it is to be revealed with fire, and the fire itself will test the quality of each man's work. If any man's work which he has built on remains, he will receive a reward. If any man's work is burned up, he will suffer loss; but he himself will be saved, yet so as through fire."
1 Corinthians 3:10-15

The second judgement is for non-Believers, the Great White Throne, which occurs after the Millennial (1,000 year reign of Christ - Revelation 20:11-15). I will explain that more when we get there; however, I want to mention this to close the loop (at a high level) on this topic.

Those appearing before the Great White Throne will be non-Believers. In other words, no Believer of the Old Testament or New Testament will appear before the Great White Throne - it is there to expose sin (truth). The choice to not accept salvation through Jesus will leave the stain of sin on that person, and remove their name from the Book of Life. They will be cast into the Lake of Fire for eternity.

Following this, John is given a vision of the coming war 'Armageddon' (Revelation 14:15).
Then we move on...

Chapter 6
The Great Tribulation - part 2

The first 3.5 years of the Tribulation created a false hope for mankind, and a stance against Christianity. The next 3.5 years, the Great Tribulation, build on that foundation:

- True Believers and Holy Spirit were removed (Rapture)
- The Antichrist has stepped into initial power
- The Antichrist finalized the seven year Israel peace treaty
- The False Prophet has displayed supernatural powers
- Jewish worship (OT) is restored at the Temple
- 144,000 Jews are marked to spread the Gospel message
- Two witnesses preached, were killed, were resurrected
- One world leadership, desires, power, influence increase
- Christian persecution and threats increase

The real agenda of the AntiChrist and False Prophet are now exposed...
The world enters the Great Tribulation (Matthew 24:20)...

The Beast takes over the global government, and the False Prophet demands everyone worship the Beast or be killed. Antichrist will vow to remove the shackles of Christianity (Psalm 2:1-6); therefore, worldly hearts rejoice in their celebration of the church's fall. Persecution will escalate: When a person commits to Jesus during this time, they are killed physically; however, their spirit is immediately in Heaven before the alter (Revelation 6:9).

The world will now recognize this agenda; more and more hearts will turn to Jesus to gain freedom from the reality created by the Beast and False Prophet. This is why some believe the total number of people saved during the Tribulation will exceed the total number saved through human history.

The seven vials of God's Wrath

As we step into Revelation 15, John sees another vision in Heaven. Seven angels, wearing white and gold are seen that will carry out the seven final plagues (Revelation 15:1). Believers (not martyrs) who remained faithful but died, are seen playing harps on a sea of water mingled with fire (Revelation 15:2). They sing songs to honor God the Father and the Son, Jesus Christ, and the judgement that is finally coming to those that oppose them.

The Temple of the Tabernacle of the Testimony that is in Heaven was opened (Revelation 15:5). The seven angels came out, and a beast handed each of them a vial full of God's wrath. The glory of God filled the Temple with smoke, and no man could enter until the seven plagues were unleashed upon the non-Believers on earth.

On earth, the first vial creates great sores upon the people that accept the Mark of the Beast and worship his image (Revelation 16:2). As the angel pours out the second vial, the sea (saltwater) becomes like the blood of a dead man; every living thing in the sea will die (Revelation 16:3). When the third vial is poured out, the rivers and fountains (fresh water) become blood (Revelation 16:4). That third angel states that mankind has shed the blood of God's saints and prophets, and now they are worthy to drink blood in return (Revelation 16:6).

John then saw the fourth angel pour the vial on the Sun, and it scorched men with fire. As they burned, they blasphemed (curse) God's name, but still would not repent to give God any glory (Revelation 16:8-9). Then the fifth angel poured his vial upon the Seat of the Beast. This filled the entire kingdom with darkness and people that were affected by the plague were gnawing at their own tongues because of the pain (Revelation 16:10-11).

The sixth angel poured out his vial on the Euphrates River, and it dries up. This event clears the way for the Kings of the East to march with their armies to Jerusalem for the great war of Armageddon (Revelation 16:12). John then saw evil spirits leap (like frogs) from the mouth of the Dragon, the Beast, and the False Prophet. These spirits were able to indoctrinate the kings of the world to gather together to battle the Lord God Almighty (Revelation 16:14). Many believe this great battle (Armageddon) will take place at the Valley of Megiddo in Israel. As we will find out later, this also is not the final war against Satan - that will be at the end of the Millennium (roughly 1,000 years later)!

Vial number seven is poured out into the air, and a great voice from the Temple in Heaven says, 'It is done' (Revelation 16:17). There is thunder, lightning, and the greatest earthquake in the history of the world (Revelation 16:18). The quake divides Jerusalem into thirds, and many great cities crumble to the ground. The earth changed so greatly that mountains and islands are physically altered (possibly so much that they will only appear as hills) (Revelation 16:18-20).

The government system under the Antichrist will be scattered; however, the Antichrist remains in command of the world government. Great hailstones, each weighing roughly one hundred pounds, fall from Heaven to the earth in a great storm. Again, mankind blasphemed God's name and would not turn to Him (Revelation 16:21).

The Government and Religion

In Heaven, one of the angels that had the vials approaches John; taking him to show him a new vision...

There is a woman (Babylon: Worldly business or trade, flourishing on selfish greed, un-Godly morals and lust filled desires), who the angel refers to as the 'Great Whore' sitting on waters (representing great multitudes of people of all nations - Revelation 17:15). The woman is full of worldly vanity; dressed in expensive apparel, covered in precious stones, and holding a golden cup full of her abominations (Revelation 17:4). This woman was drunk from the joy of the killing of the Believers of God throughout time (Revelation 17:6). She had a writing on her head (Revelation 17:5):

"Mystery, Babylon the Great, the mother of harlots and abominations of the earth." - Revelation 17:5

This is the great city of Babylon that is promoted by the Antichrist and False Prophet. She has seduced the kings of the earth, and many people with her lies, temporary worldly pleasures, and false hope of victory over God (Revelation 17:2). This woman was sitting on a scarlet colored beast (world government), led by the Beast (Antichrist). They are so in sync with each other, that they appear to move as one entity (Revelation 17:3).

The beast was covered in blasphemous names against God, and had seven heads (mountains) which represents Rome (many believe the Beast will revive the Great Roman Empire), that sits on seven mountains (Revelation 17:9). This 'Revived Roman Empire' is also believed by some to be the wounded head that was thought to be dead, but was revived (Revelation 13:3)

This beast also had 10 horns (kings), which represent 10 kings without kingdoms, but instead are led to believe that they share the reign of power under the leadership of the Beast (Revelation 17:12-13). They will give their power and strength (armies and resources) to the Beast as his own. The Beast will use all of these resources to make war against the Lamb, the Lord of Lords, and King of Kings (Jesus). (Revelation 17:14)

Babylon - the unbelieving world

A very impressive and powerful angel, whose glory enlightened the earth, came down from Heaven to John on the earth (Revelation 18:1). The angel says Babylon has fallen, and has become the dwelling place for devils, foul spirits, every unclean and hateful bird. Unbelieving leaders have joined in her deceit, greed, lusts, and have become wealthy through their relationships and dealings with her and each other (Revelation 18:2-3).

Another angel then came out and pleaded for people to turn from Babylon and come out from the city to avoid God's wrath. He explains that God remembers their actions, and selfish iniquities, and will bring His wrath and plagues on them for their sins. The reward for their choices will be twice as bad as their treatment of God through history. Since she has lived in worldly luxuries and vanities, she will receive torment and sorrow (Revelation 18:4-7).

The Lord's judgement is strong on Babylon, and His wrath will be poured out on her in one day (Revelation 18:8). There will be death, mourning, famine, plagues, and utterly burned with fire. When this happens, the Kings of the earth will cry as they see the smoke and flames rising up. They will feel sorrow for they cannot buy and sell their products any longer (Revelation 18:9-11). They will lose money, precious earthly possessions, animals and slave labor (Revelation 18:12-19).

In Heaven, there is rejoicing! God has finally avenged the holy apostles and prophets for the treatment they received, and blood they shed. There will be no more trade, music, crafts; not even a candle's light will shine in this worldly city. A mighty angel casts a giant mill stone into the sea:

'Thus, with violence shall that great city Babylon be thrown down, and shall be found no more at all' - Revelation 18:21

After this, Heaven erupts; giving praise, honor and glory to God and to the Lord. The Great Whore is judged, and the blood of His prophets avenged (Revelation 18:20-24). The 24 elders and four beasts fell down before God's throne and worshipped saying Amen, Alleluia, for the Lord God omnipotent reigns! (Revelation 19:4-6).

The marriage of the Lamb (Jesus) and Bride (church)

This is a great moment in Heaven, the marriage of the Lamb (Jesus) and His Bride (the church). Jesus has paid for every sin on the Cross of Calvary, He became our sin (2 Corinthians 5:21). His finished work has cleansed us by our faith (Acts 15:9), to be an acceptable Bride for Him this day. Only through Him, are we (the church body) able to now stand in our gown of righteousness (Revelation 19:8) as a Bride for the Bridegroom (Jesus) at this ceremony. Heaven celebrates as this wedding proceeds, and each member in attendance feels true blessing (Revelation 19:9).

John tries to worship the angel, but is rebuked. The angel is a fellow servant of the Lord, like John (Revelation 19:10). This is a great lesson: We are to worship God, and serve Him only (Luke 4:8).

The second coming of Christ will bring a lot of emotions, and differing views as to what this means for the world going forward...

The Second Coming of Christ - the Messiah King

Heaven opens to reveal a white horse with Jesus Christ sitting on it. His eyes were flames of fire (judgement) and He has many crowns on His head (power and authority). His clothing was dipped in blood and He is called 'the Word of God' (Revelation 19:11-13, John 1:14)! Some believe the blood represents vengeance for the blood of the saints, and His own suffering; while others believe it symbolizes the bloody judgement that is about to fall on Satan's army. Christ's armies (angels) in Heaven follow Him, sitting on white horses, in clean white clothing, ready for battle.

The Second Coming of Christ - The church

Even in the post-Tribulation Rapture theory, the dead Believers would be resurrected at this time. The three Rapture options actually converge at this point in time, so that does help pull things back together and get everyone on the same path. That said, there are a couple of views as to what role the church will play when Christ returns. This really comes down to where you believe the church will physically be.

I would say the most common theory is that Jesus returns with His angel armies, and all Believers (throughout all of time) will reign with Him in the Millennial Kingdom for 1,000 years. That would be the saints (Zechariah 14:5), Christians (2 Timothy 2:12), and Tribulation martyrs (Revelation 20:4) as well as the 144,000 sealed Jews. All will then enter the Millennium and live on earth through the 1,000 years in peace. They would give praise and honor to Jesus as the Messiah King, and evangelize the truth throughout all of the nations.

Another view (which I personally believe) is that only angels return with Christ to face off against Satan, and his rebel angels (Revelation 19:19). All Old Testament saints are resurrected (Ezekiel 37:9), and they will be an 'exceeding great army' (Ezekiel 37:10). Their focus will be to defend Jerusalem against the human armies of the Beast. Jesus will take His place as the Messiah.

The Tribulation martyrs will be resurrected (Revelation 20:4) to join the Old Testament saints, under the resurrected King David (Ezekiel 37:24), and reign with Christ in Jerusalem (Revelation 20:4-6). The 144,000 will re-establish the twelve Jewish Tribes of Judah as they were in the Old Testament. The tribes of Joseph and Judah will be united together as one nation (Ezekiel 37:15-22).

The church is in the new Jerusalem (or perhaps the church *IS* the new Jerusalem itself), which remains in Heaven until it is brought to the new Earth at the end of the Millennium (Revelation 21:2). Clear as mud, right? I'll dig into more details when we enter the Millennium and hopefully this will make a little more sense...

The Second Coming of Christ - Jews / Muslims

This is closing out the chapter of God's story for the church (on our current earth - see Revelation 21:1). God has offered prophesies, promises, and blessings to Israel that have yet to be fulfilled - and will be fulfilled in the Millennium. This is the point of the Millennium: Jesus as the Lion of Judah, the Messiah King, reigning in His Kingdom, to keep His promises and bless His people, Israel.

The traditional Jewish and Muslim faithful do not accept that Jesus was the Messiah (John 5:31-57); but instead state He was a teacher (Jews) or Prophet (Muslims). Jewish Leaders used Jesus's claim to be the Son of God in their prosecution to Pilate; demanding His crucifixion for blasphemy (Luke 23:21). Then, their self-serving desires led them to claim Caesar as their *ONLY* King (John 19:15)! (They didn't understand this was God's predestined event, and He was using their hardened hearts for His good!)

Jerusalem will be very interesting to watch when Jesus returns. Jews, Christians, and Muslims have all worshipped in Jerusalem since the Mandate for Religious Freedom (1948) and Reunification Agreement (1967). However, Jews and Muslims do not acknowledge the Christian church, which worships Jesus as the Son of God.

So, how will these faiths respond when they see Jesus returning in the clouds? We will have wait and see...

Today, faithful Orthodox Jews are preparing for the Messiah's coming (see "The Temple Institute" for more details). When Jesus returns as King, they will *then* realize that Jesus *IS* their Messiah! Muslims will also remain through the Millennium; however, I believe many will hold strong to their faith. Many religions/faiths will not accept Jesus for who he is and will probably be part of the final rebellion (both in Revelation 19:20-21, and 20:8-9). All who do not accept Jesus will be cast into the Lake of Fire for eternity (Revelation 20:15).

NOTE:
There is a group of Jewish people that also accept that Jesus is the Messiah today. This is a little challenging to understand, but they are 100% Jewish, and 100% Christian. They maintain the Jewish faith, and look forward to the return of Jesus as their Messiah to fulfill the promises and blessings to their people (see "Jews for Jesus" for more details).

Armageddon

The return of Christ with His angel army, and on to Armageddon (Revelation 19:11). The descriptions gets a little gruesome and even sadistic; but we must remember, this is God's wrath on all sin, through all time.

On earth, the truth is proclaimed through the Word of God (sword from His mouth), and this will destroy the nations (most likely referring to leaders and governments). Jesus will be very strict in His discipline, enforcing His authority with a rod of iron. The fierce wrath of God will squash sin like grapes in a winepress (Revelation 19:15).

The great rulers of the Beast's kingdom will fall, and the great number of dead bodies will be scattered throughout the land. God calls on the birds of the air to come and feast on their carcasses, referring to this as a great feast. The birds will eat the bodies of all men and even their horses or animals used in the battle (Revelation 19:17,18,21).

The Beast is furious, and his pride defies the reality that is evident: Prophecy is being fulfilled. He gathers all of the defiant angels, and they charge into battle against Christ and His army! They are utterly defeated.

The Beast and False prophet, that deceived, oppressed, and strong-armed so many into eternal damnation, are cast alive into the Lake of Fire to burn for all eternity (Revelation 19:20). They will no longer torment Christians, nor the faithful of Israel. But free will and sin will remain through the Millennium.

An angel then descends from Heaven with a key to the Bottomless Pit and a massive chain. This angel takes hold of Satan and throws him in the Bottomless Pit, securing him for 1,000 years with an unbreakable seal. He will be set loose again at the end of the Millennium; but, for the next 1,000 years, he will not be able to deceive anyone (the nations) throughout the earth (Revelation 20:3).

This is the end of the 70th week of Daniel's prophecy (Daniel 9:24-27). The church's dispensation is completed. God's focus returns to His people, Israel; blessings, promises, and deliverance through their Messiah King, Jesus Christ! Amen!

Chapter 7
The Millennium (Millennial Kingdom)

L et's recap. There is so much that has happened, and I want to ensure we understand where this leaves us as we enter this new dispensation. Remember, the church (Grace) dispensation is a parenthesis following the 69th week of Daniel's prophecy where Messiah is killed or removed ('cut off' - Daniel 9:25-26).

The Rapture removed the current church (Revelation 4:1), and the seven year peace treaty initiates the Tribulation. This resumes Daniel's prophecy for Israel to complete the 70 week (Daniel 9:27); setting up Jesus to take His role as Messiah for Israel. In addition, I believe the Holy Spirit will once again interact with Israel similar to the Old Testament (entering and departing - 1 Samuel 16:13-23).

So in essence, the Tribulation is God reshaping and cleansing the earth; a dispensational transition from the church back to the people of Israel...

Where are they now?

Let's take a look at where each individual or group is now located, according to the interpretations I have shared. God the Father is in Heaven. The church is in Heaven. I believe Christ's angel army will return to Heaven as Satan is sealed in the bottomless pit.

On earth, Jesus has now returned to occupy His throne as Messiah of Israel. Martyrs for Jesus will now sit in seats of authority and judgement. The 144,000 Jewish faithful, with the mark of God in their forehead (Luke 12:32, Revelation 14:1), will spread the Gospel to all nations.

What about those that are not Israel?

Some assume that all non-Believers will join Satan's army to fight against Jesus (Armageddon); however, scripture does not state that. Jesus and His army will fight Satan and his army (whomever that may be). We can assume some non-Believers will not join Satan, and will not accept the 'Mark of the Beast'. It is assumed they will remain and enter the Millennium as modern day Gentiles.

We can also assume that not all Christians will be killed during the Tribulation. I believe they will be raptured to Heaven before the Millennium. The rapture of Believers will start at the Rapture event (Revelation 4:1), continue with immediate rapture at death through the seven year Tribulation, and conclude with the first resurrection at the end of the Tribulation (Revelation 20:5).

Resurrection of the Jews

With the Christian church raptured, the focus on earth is Israel. There are many promises to Israel that need to be fulfilled by Jesus, as He takes His throne as the Messiah; the Lion of Judah. Finally, this is what the Jewish people have been longing for!

Ezekiel 37 shows a restoration of Israel - bringing dry bones to life. I believe this refers to a literal resurrection of the full nation of Israel (Revelation 20:5-6). Jesus will be King, and David will be resurrected as their prince (Ezekiel 37:24-25).

In addition, this resurrection of Israel also separates those that have been faithful to Him, and those who have not. Jesus spoke of this judgement, commonly referred to as the judgement of the sheep and goats (Matthew 25:31-46). The sheep (faithful - right hand) will continue on to the Millennial Kingdom prepared for them, to receive the rest of their promises and blessings (Matthew 25:34). The goats (unfaithful - left hand) will be cast into the Lake of Fire (Matthew 25:41).

What does daily life look like in the Millennium?

To understand what this Millennial Kingdom will be like, we must turn back to the Old Testament. There are several prophets that spoke of this Kingdom in their writings. First of all, Jesus will reign as King and David will be resurrected as the Prince of the Kingdom (Isaiah 9:6-7, Jeremiah 30:9). They will reign over the house of Jacob (Israel) forever (Luke 1:32-33) from the (third) Temple in Jerusalem (Ezekiel 40-48).

There will be peace and prosperity throughout the world (Isaiah 2:2-4, Amos 9:13). As with many times of peace and prosperity through history, there is a population boom.

Many will travel to Jerusalem to eat and visit with the prophets (Matthew 8:11). In addition, there will be plenty of quality food and wines prepared for everyone to enjoy. Jesus will wipe away tears, destroy fears, and destroy the veil (lies and deceit) that has covered the earth for so long (Isaiah 25).

This is a general statement, for there will still be free will, and people will rebel against Jesus and David's leadership and authority. They will be corrected, but some will still not repent, and their defiance will culminate at the end of the Millennium, in the great final war!

Although death still exists, all of the earth will enjoy much longer lives (Isaiah 65:19-20). This will be much like the life spans that were seen in the book of Genesis; for instance, Methusela, who lived to be 969 years old (Genesis 5:27). A young person will be 100 years old, and if they don't reach that age, they will be considered 'cursed' (Isaiah 65:19-20).

Temple sacrifices restored: Christ's atonement for Sin

This can create a bit of a question within Christian theology. Why? Because in the New Testament, we are taught that Christ's one-time sacrifice has paid the price for our sins (Colossians 1:14, 2:17). So let's dig in a little here...

The purpose of the temple sacrifices (Leviticus) were, in essence, a daily reminder of the reality of sin. The key point is that the sacrifices were ongoing, so this only atoned for the sins that were confessed at the time. The confession was made, and their sin was placed on the animal - transferring the 'curse' to the animal to be killed. This had to be repeated daily, monthly, yearly; as sin continued in people's lives and required atonement.

Another key point: No work could be completed that would atone for sins. Their faith in God is what was counted as righteousness (Genesis 15:6, Romans 4:3); whereas, the ritual was simply obedience. David defines this clearly in his prayer to God after committing adultery with Bathsheba (Psalm 51:16-17).

A sacrifice in action alone, without faith, does not appeal to God. I would go as far as to say, it is not accepted by God (Genesis 4:5). This is also the case with baptism, communion, etc. All of these are personal actions done in obedience as Believers. However, if done without faith, they truly mean nothing. As stated previously, works will not produce salvation (Ephesians 2:8-9).

The Apostle Paul states clearly that sacrifices could not accomplish what Jesus's blood sacrifice did for us (Hebrews 9:12-14). Just as with the sacrifices in the Old Testament, Jesus became a curse, so the curse could be put to death (Galatians 3:13-15).

This payment was required for God's justice to be fulfilled, for the price of sin is death. Thankfully, that price was willingly paid in full for our freedom by Jesus Christ, on the cross of Calvary (Romans 6:23). More important here is that Jesus paid that price once and for all (Hebrews 10:10).

*So, why do we need sacrifices again
in the new Kingdom?*

Temple sacrifices restored: What each means

We have only spoken of one sacrifice so far, the sin sacrifice. Remember, there were multiple sacrifices in the Old Testament, each having their respective meaning. So, let's take a quick look at the sacrifices to hopefully understand why some of these are still relevant today (or, in the Millennial Kingdom).

The first sacrifice was actually in the Garden of Eden (Genesis 3:21). Adam and Eve sinned. God exposed their sin to them through questions, which led to their confession (repentance). God then killed an animal (blood sacrifice for sin - atonement) and used the skin to cover them (addressing or correcting the exposed sin).

Then we see various references to sacrifices with Cain and Abel, distinctions between what is clean or unclean, and details about which first fruits are to be used. As for sacrifices, there are different views on why Cain's sacrifice was rejected. What we can take from scripture is that all sacrifices must be done in faith. It can be assumed that Cain's heart was not right with God, probably seeking notoriety vs. freely giving to God.

Let's review each of the sacrifices...

- The burnt offering
  (Leviticus 1; 6:8-13; 8:18-21; 16:24)
This was to express worship and devotion to God, and to address unintentional sin: A blood offering was made from a washed bull, bird, or a ram without blemish. God's portion was the meat, bones, and organs - burned, and the ashes scattered outside of the camp. The Levites were given the skins to sell for the Temple needs.

- The grain offering
  (Leviticus 2; 6:14-23)

This offering was a thanksgiving of God's goodwill and provision from that person or household. The person would prepare a cake or bread made from the best grain of their fields, which was burned upon the altar. In addition, a drink offering, roughly one quart of wine, was poured into the fire on the altar. The priests were given a portion of this offering, but they had to eat it within the court of the Tabernacle.

- The peace offering
  (Leviticus 3; 7:11-34)

This was an offering for peace and fellowship consisting of unleavened baked goods with oil, leavened bread and an animal sacrifice. God's portion - the fat, kidneys, and lobe of liver - were burned (anyone eating these would be cut off from the people). The remainder was prepared and eaten within two days, and the leftovers were burned on the third day. Priests used the breast and right foreleg as a wave offering (side to side motion) and heave offering (up and down motion), and sprinkled blood in that place.

- The sin (willing transgressions/iniquity) offering
  (Leviticus 4; 5:1-13; 6:24-30; 8:14-17; 16:3-22)

This offering was for the atonement of sins, or for touching anything deemed 'unclean'. The first part was to confess the sin (Leviticus 5:5); then, the best item (available to the offerer) from an accepted list was brought to the Priest: Lamb (sheep) or kid (goat), two turtledoves or pigeons, 1/10 an ephah (bushel) of flour. The Priest would burn this, and the person would make amends as needed (repent and correct what they could).

Note: When Aaron was offering for his, and his household's sins, it appears he would bring a young bull for the sin offering (Leviticus 8:14).

- The trespass (unknown, unwillingly sins) offering
  (Leviticus 5:14-19; 6:1-7; 7:1-6)

The purpose of this offering was for unintentional sins. This offering was exclusively a ram without blemish. God's portion - fat, kidneys, liver - were burned as an offering. The remainder was prepared and eaten inside the Court of the Tabernacle.

One additional note for clarification: As detailed above, there is a difference between sins that are willingly (knowingly) committed (requiring a sin offering) and those unwillingly committed (requiring a trespass offering). David also highlights the two types of sin (Psalm 51:2-3, 9); willfully sinning (known and acknowledged), and unknown trespasses (ongoing and unintentional).

We now have an understanding of the sacrifices in the Old Testament, and their respective purpose. So then, what would still be required in the Millennial Kingdom?

Temple sacrifices restored: The Millennium

To start, just because Jesus and David are on their thrones in Jerusalem, doesn't mean sin has been removed from our flesh (Romans 8:3). As a matter of fact, Zechariah states that Christ will sit as both King and High Priest, and there will be harmony between the two (Zechariah 6:13). So, if the finished work of Christ on the Cross has paid the price for all sin (history, present, and future - 1 John 2:2), why would we need Jesus to be the High Priest?

This is what was mentioned earlier, that sin (and death) still exists, and people will continue to sin through the Millennium. That said, the Millennial sacrifices are not about forgiveness of sins or purchasing salvation; that is through Jesus Christ alone. There are a few views on this...

Just as the sacrifices in the Old Testament looked forward to Christ's sacrifice, some think the sacrifices in the Millennium will look back, to honor Christ's sacrifice. Also, they believe this shows both sorrow and joy, as they consider their forefathers that rejected the truth, as well as the privilege of clearly seeing it today (in the Millennium). This would fall in line with many customs of Israel, such as setting up stones, etc., for remembering events or people. I can accept this as a viable reasoning.

Another view is to look at the specific meanings of each sacrifice to determine what would still be needed and honored by God. The first three offerings - burnt, grain and peace - were all honoring to God from His faithful people. It would make sense that these three still remain in the Millennium. The last two were for the sins of the individual or household; so those are no longer needed... right?

Either of the two views make sense in my mind as both would acknowledge the finished work of Jesus Christ, and His role as King, High Priest, Lord and Savior. All we know for sure, is that the Temple will be set up for Israel as stated by Ezekiel, Isaiah, Jeremiah, Zechariah, and Malachi, and sacrifices will resume in the Millennial Kingdom.

The end of the Millennial Kingdom: Judgements

So, life will proceed through the Millennium and salvation, as always, will come only through faith in God and His Son. Now we move forward to the conclusion of this 1,000 year reign of Christ. The population has grown, many becoming faithful, and others becoming more and more defiant to God.

Satan will be released from the bottomless pit (Revelation 20:7). He will use his influence to deceive those who are against God to believe they can overthrow Him by force. Satan will gather them, a huge amount of people (uncountable - Revelation 20:8) to battle Jesus and those faithful to Him in Jerusalem. God will then send fire down from Heaven to consume them all, except for Satan (Revelation 20:9).

Jesus will then cast Satan into the Lake of Fire, where the Beast and the False Prophet are, to be tormented forever and ever (Revelation 20:10). Notice the wording: scripture says where the Beast and False Prophet *ARE*. This shows that they are still there, and assuming that they are eternal beings, they will literally be tortured for all eternity.

Next, Jesus will set up His Great White Throne. You will remember that all of Israel was resurrected, so non-Believers in that group were already cast into the Lake of Fire 1,000 years earlier. Now, all of the remaining non-Believers from throughout history of the world will be resurrected to face their judgement (Revelation 20:11-15).

Jesus will refer to multiple books, but really only two categories from what scripture shows. One set of books is the listing of people's actions or 'works' through their lifetime. These will be announced publicly, which will show they have sinned and are accountable for their sins. The other book, is the Book of Life...

Jesus will open the Book of Life, which contains the names of people of faith through the history of mankind. Those who have not chosen faith in God or accepted His Son, Jesus, will be cast into the Lake of Fire (Revelation 20:15).

There is some debate on whether those condemned will burn for eternity in the Lake of Fire. Some believe that the fire burns eternally, and that this is deserved judgement for sin. Others believe that since God is Love, and would rather see sin destroyed forever, they will be consumed by flames instead of ongoing torment. Since this has nothing to do with salvation, either way this is interpreted, sin is no more, and will never be again.

Death and Hell still exist through the Millennium. People will die (Isaiah 65:20); Believers will go to Heaven, and non-Believers will still be sent to Hell until the time of their judgement before the Great White Throne (Revelation 20:13).

After non-Believers are resurrected to judgement, Hell will be empty, and there will be more more death; therefore, they are also cast into the Lake of Fire (Revelation 20:14). Satan, the Beast, the False prophet, non-believing Israel, non-believing world, death, and hell are all dealt with - FOREVER!

The final judgements are complete.
We now move on to the finale...

Chapter 8
Eternity: New Heaven, new Earth

Well, there you have it. God's plan for how He will address sin, Satan, and the unbelieving world we live in... at least my view of this, in a nutshell. The only remaining beings are Millennial Believers on the earth, the church (new Jerusalem), and heavenly creatures (angels, beasts) which are all in Heaven.

So now, God finishes reshaping His creation, once and for all. John states that the old Heaven and old Earth (as they are today), are 'passed away', and there is no more sea (Revelation 21:1). This may refer to a cleansing by fire (Isaiah 66:16, 2 Peter 3:7) through judgement and the Lake of Fire.

Okay...so what will that be like?

Eternity: What will life be like?

This is a very interesting question to ask people of all ages and maturity levels in their Christian walk. Most people honestly don't know what to expect. Many people simply accept that it will be love, and sin-free, and that is enough. Others reply, 'It's Heaven... how could we even imagine? All I know is it'll be great.' Most who have not studied this topic agree that it will be vastly different. To some extent, I believe we all think it would be different, right?

But again...what does scripture say it will be like?

Eternity: The new heavens (atmosphere)

The 'old heavens' are replaced with a 'new heaven' (Revelation 21:1). I feel it is safe to say the 'heaven' referred to here is the heaven that is tied to the earth (our atmosphere), vs. the eternal place of God the Father. scripture doesn't speak much to what the 'new heaven' will be like.

In Revelation, John is shown that there will be no need for a sun or moon, since the glory of Christ will be the light forever more. Since the glory of Christ shines continually, there will be no night (Revelations 21:25, 22:5). The brightest, clearest light (Revelation 22:11), but a light that will not hurt your eyes and no sunburns!

There are no verses that speak to whether we will even need air to breathe. We cannot determine if there will be oxygen, carbon monoxide, or even if our new bodies will have lungs, hearts or even blood for that matter. It is assumed that the new bodies will not require the atmosphere that we currently require today. Since there is no more death...what would be the purpose, right?

Eternity: The new Earth

The 'old Heaven and Earth' will be replaced with a 'new Heaven and Earth' (a rebirth of His Creation). This is fulfillment of God's promises and Isaiah's prophecies (Isaiah 65:17, 66:22). Also, the curse that God placed on His Creation (Genesis 3:17), because of man's sin (Romans 8:18), is removed (Revelation 22:3). This will be like it was in the beginning with the Garden of Eden (Genesis 1:28-2:25); peaceful, innocent, sin-free, death-free, self-sufficient.

Some believe this 'rebirth' (Revelation 22:1) will be a total destruction since the old Earth and heavens have been tainted by sin. But, considering the scenario that I have shared, people will still be living on the earth (Resurrected Israel, and the Faithful through the Millennium), how would they be delivered? Would there be some kind of 'ark' to deliver them? Could this be the new Jerusalem? Although I won't state that's *not* a possible scenario (Matthew 19:26), there is no scriptural backing to those theories.

Personally, I believe this will be a reshaping of the earth; a continuation of the changes already seen. Remember, a great earthquake already reshaped (or removed) mountains and moved (or removed) islands. The waters were also destroyed; first turned to blood, then dried up during the Tribulation. Apparently, they are not restored again on the new earth for there are no more seas (oceans). This is huge, considering water covers nearly 75% of earth today.

So then, we can also assume there will be no sea life (animals or plants). I feel like that is a safe assumption at this point since there is no mention of animals at all (land or sea) in the new Heaven and new Earth. There is a river spoken of that flows from the Throne of God and of the Lamb, but this is stated to be a river of 'water of life' (to be covered in new Jerusalem section). I believe this river is not the same as the water we know and need for survival today.

Eternity: Old temple, old Jerusalem

One prominent component of worship for Israel, and Jewish people through all of the ages, has been the Temple. This will have been constructed and destroyed two times in history, and rebuilt again the third time going into the Tribulation. Even if this temple is not destroyed during the final war in the Millennium, it is assumed it will no longer be used (Revelation 21:22).

In fact, the city of Jerusalem that we know today will not be the eternal city for Christ's eternal reign. The former things are all passed away, and He has made all things new (Revelation 21:4-5). In fact, Isaiah states we will not even remember the former things (Isaiah 65:17).

The new Jerusalem is the eternal city where all of God's faithful will dwell with him forever. Let's take a look at how scripture describes this new city...

Eternity: New Jerusalem

The new Jerusalem descends out of Heaven, a bride ordained for her Husband (Revelation 21:2). This is a key statement. Remember back to the Marriage of the Lamb at the end of the Tribulation just before Christ returns. The title of 'bride' refers to the church, and the 'bridegroom' refers to Jesus. This would then be referring to the church (bride) and Jesus (bride's husband).

Also, the angel speaking to John refers to the Bride as the Lamb's wife (Revelation 22:9), which would be the church's title now since the Marriage of the Lamb. This is my reasoning to state the church is considered to be in the new Jerusalem as it descends to Jesus.

This city is described (Revelation 21:10-27) as having a great wall, roughly 216 feet tall and made of jasper. It has 12 gates which look like pearls, and contain the names of the 12 tribes of Israel. The wall has 12 foundations, each with the name of an apostle of Christ and garnished with precious stones. This represents the joint faith of Old Testament and New Testament saints.

The shape of the city is a square or possibly a triangle (like a pyramid); each side measuring 1,500 miles (equal height, length, and width). John sees this city in which the streets appear to be the purest gold, and clear like glass. There is no temple, for God the Father, and Jesus Christ the Son are the open temple for all people.

Eternity: Living in love

The only people who will have access to the new Jerusalem are the faithful Believers from throughout history (Revelation 21:7). Only those who are written in the Lamb's Book of Life will be able to enter (Revelation 21:27). The nations of Believers have full access to bring honor and glory to God at all times (Revelation 21:25).

God shall embrace each of His faithful with love and compassion. He will wipe away all tears, and there will be no more sorrow, death, crying, or even pain. From His throne, He will make all things new, and offer the water of life freely to anyone (Revelation 21:4).

From the throne will flow a pure river of 'water of life', crystal clear (Revelation 22:1), which God gives freely to anyone as desired (Revelation 21:6). On each side of the river, there is the Tree of Life. It is unclear if this is one tree that spans across the river to both sides, or if there will be more than one Tree of Life in the new Paradise. This tree bares twelve fruits every month, and the leaves are for (most likely) therapeutic 'healing' for the nations (Revelation 22:2).

John mentions that Believers will have a seal on their forehead that will show they are God's people. I am not sure if this is a visible seal or if this is more symbolic. For instance, the Jewish people strap a small leather box (called a tefillin) to their forehead and upper arm. This box contains verses of the Torah and is placed there to be at the forefront of their thoughts. God will be in the forefront of our minds in eternity, so that could be what is meant here.

Once last thing to mention is that Believers will see God's face. This is the first time that any human will have ever seen the face of God and lived (Exodus 33:20). This also is another promise that was made by Jesus, that the pure of heart would see God (Matthew 5:8). Oh, how amazing it will be to see God face to face, and live in an eternal environment of perfect love!

Final warnings to all mankind (Revelation 22:6-21)

John is then told of final warnings to share with the readers of the book he is writing (Revelation). Jesus will come quickly, and when He arrives we will be judged as we are (Revelation 22:11). There will not be time to plead for forgiveness (Matthew 7:23), or to then try to further your faith (Matthew 25:1-13). Jesus is the one and only way (John 14:6), He is the door to Salvation (John 10:9), and that door will be shut (Luke 13:25).

Blessed are the faithful and obedient Believers, who upon His return are found doing His work for the Kingdom (Matthew 24:46). They will have full access into the new Jerusalem, and interact directly with God the Father and His Son, Jesus (Revelation 22:14). God invites all to come (Revelation 22:17), and curses anyone who will add or take away from the truth of scripture (Revelation 22:19).

Amazing to imagine...

If you want to have an interesting conversation, sit down with a few Believers and ask them what eternity will be like. It's incredibly hard to imagine life without the basics of our normal existence. Will our new bodies require food, water, oxygen, exercise, or even sleep? There will be no more day and night, death, money, jobs, sickness, tears, hate, or even disrespect...all need is gone.

I asked my wife, Linda, this question, and I loved her response. She said, "How about something even more basic, like time? What are we going to do with all of our time?" It was something I had not considered; but it was a huge concept once I let the wheels start turning in my head...think about it...

We schedule our days to be as efficient as possible, making the most of the time we have been given. Work, school classes, church services, study groups, sports events, travel schedules, etc. all require very precise and consistent timing. Business professionals pay very close attention to time, and even create training courses on time management. Many families have meal times, bed times, quiet times, and most people look forward to "down" time. Time, or to be more precise, the lack of time, will be a huge difference in our lives.

When I asked my kids for their thoughts, they took a different route. They were wondering who we would know, and what relationships will be like? Great questions.

Matthew and Mark both quote Jesus as saying we will be like the angels, and we will not marry each other (Matthew 22:30, Mark 12:25). With no marriage, it can be assumed that there will be no need (or even desire) for physical intimacy, no new pregnancies, no new children. That's not to say there won't be people of all earthly ages in new bodies. For instance, if someone passes young, or even in the womb, what age will they be in the new Paradise?

Consider how we relate to each other in our normal platonic relationships. I am assuming we will have no issues with self-esteem, image, jealousy, judgement, ridicule, praise (for each other), etc. When we consider the world we live in today, we see constant reports of hate, racism, arrogance, disrespect and privilege. But in this environment, I believe it will be pure love and respect for each other. Quite a change.

A challenge...

I want you to think about the world we live in today. As you consider the last few pages of reading, do you feel you will miss some things in your life today? What things will you be happy to see removed from your life, and our world today?

I want to encourage you to have this discussion with other Believers. I feel it will spur interesting conversation, and self-discovery... Then, we'll turn our attention to 2020, and how things are lining up with biblical prophecies.

Chapter 9
What are the signs in 2020

We have laid out a reasonable storyline for the End Times based on scriptures from both the Old Testament and New Testament. This took us through the final three dispensations of Christian Eschatology: The Tribulation, Millennium, and Eternal Future. We reviewed events in both Heaven and Earth, and the effects those events may have on the people living on earth.

Now, let's look at the practical application of all of this. What do we see specifically in our world today that shows we are heading into these End Times? What are some examples in today's world that appear to line up now, or at least are positioning us to line up, with the warnings and signs that Jesus warned us about in Matthew 24?

What is reality (subjective vs. objective)

To understand what is happening around us, we must confirm that we understand actual truth. Today's world is filled with sources that are determined to get you to believe 'their' view regarding situations. Mainstream Media (MSM), social media, and even political and religious teachings are influencing the way we perceive reality today. So where to start? The answer is truth.

I have used the word 'reality' many times in my writing...why? Let's look at the definition of 'truth' from one of my favorite sources:

'Conformity to fact or reality; exact accordance with that which is, or has been, or shall be. The truth of history constitutes its whole value. We rely on the truth of the scriptural prophecies.' - 1828 Webster's Dictionary

So, reality equals truth. Pretty simple. However, reality is not always the truth that we want to hear. Unfortunately, journalistic integrity has much to be desired in recent years. Reporting is more commonly biased - writing to please people (pleasing itching ears) instead of writing truth, as warned about in the Bible (2 Timothy 4:3).

This is a huge problem, and causes great divisive walls between people, even starting within our own homes. The source of our information for truth is **SO** important, which is again, why I point back to the Holy Bible as my foundation for truth. I fully believe every situation and individual action can be associated to a principle that is taught in scripture; whether good or bad.

Always seek truth. (Ephesians 4:15, John 16:13)

Disclaimer

I want to be very clear on the information that I am about to share. The people and events that I reference either have occurred, or are occurring at this time. My intention is not to put a particular name on any character; instead, I want to point out the actions and events that seem to be aligning us with End Times prophecies. People *will be* mentioned; but to be honest, the puppets are usually those who are seen, while the puppet master remains in the dark.

UN, NWO, WCPA: One world Government

The Antichrist will form a one world government (Psalm 2:2). You may have heard of the 'New World Order' (NWO), the 'United Nations' (UN), World Constitution and Parliament Association (World Government Agenda), Committee to Frame a World Constitution, or the World Association for World Federation (just to name a few). Or perhaps you've heard 'rogue' terms such as: Collective security; interdependence, world law, or rule of law to promote global institutions. A one world government is being pursued - that is reality.

The UN is set up to 'host negotiations for governments; to find areas of agreement and solve problems together' (from their website). In theory, the UN is a great option for nations to come together and resolve issues. That said, they have always had a strong bias against Israel, siding many times with their majority which is the Arab (anti-Semitic) nations. This group is not fully dominating in their power or authority today; however, they have the potential to morph into a very strong and influential World Governing body.

The NWO is stated to be a myth; however, many people have spoken of this as part of their agenda. Woodrow Wilson referred to a 'League of Nations' (1920), then post-war reports referred to his efforts as a 'New World Order'. FDR and even Hitler used the term 'New World Order' in 1928. H.G. Wells wrote *The New World Order* in 1940. It is reality.

More recently, George H. Bush, George Soros, Mikhail Gorbachev and others have specifically referred to the term 'New World Order'. Reporters have also used the term 'Obama's New World Order' when referring to Barack Obama's attempts to meet with other nations while he was President of the United States, and even after.

Although I will not name a specific person as the Antichrist (many have tried), I personally believe the Antichrist may be born and living on the earth we live in today. The world is seeking liberal domination and peace, so it is primed for this person to step in and be welcomed.

So let's see what governments are doing in today's world...

Governing/Leadership actions to promote this

The Coronavirus (Covid-19) that originated in China, has been a global pandemic, which is very real. The concern around leadership is based on actions before this outbreak and actions since its inception. As you review Covid-19 data, always remember the fact that both the Center for Disease Control (CDC) and World Health Organization (WHO) stated coronavirus was first reported in Wuhan, China on December 31, 2019.

Case and point; In October 2019, a session (Event 201) was an exercise held to agree on a response in case a global virus outbreak occurred. Interesting note - this included the Chinese Center for Disease Control and Prevention, Bill Gates, and others that have become mouthpieces on how this pandemic should have been handled. Gordon Brown (UN Special Envoy for Global Education) called for a 'global government to cope with a pandemic like this', and also stated, 'I feel the New World Order is emerging'.

Do you feel it is odd that this became such a 'hot' global topic just three months before this global outbreak? Coincidence? Perhaps, but statements do *seem* to point to this type of incident ushering in a 'New World Order'. Similar reports have led conspiracy theorists to claim the virus was purposely released to push that very agenda. As much as I truly hope world leaders would not release this virus on purpose, power and pride has led to many decisions and/or events that leave mass casualties in their wake. It is tragic, it is reality, and only a small taste of the Spirit of Antichrist (2 Thessalonians 2:3-12, 1 John 4:3).

In addition, governing bodies are meeting at an event called the 'World Government Summit' (actual event name), hosted in Dubai. Their mission statement is quite appealing: 'Ushering in a new era of responsibility and accountability to serve citizens better through inclusion'. Then, their vision statement: 'To become the global platform for shaping future government'. Once again, promoting a one world governing entity - this is reality.

Let's also not forget that the Antichrist (Leader of the one world Government), and the False Prophet (Leader of the one world Religion) will be working together. The UN (one representation of world government today) has shown great adoration for Pope Francis's push for Socialism and Globalism. The Pope would be a key ally to global domination: The religious leader of nearly 72 million people proclaiming to be Catholics. That's huge influence.

Catholicism: Paving the way for a one world religion

I want to be state clearly that I do not believe that everyone in the Catholic Church is promoting anti-Christian views, or are 'minions of Satan'! I have personally had many discussions with Catholic Church members who are very concerned about statements and actions of the current Pope, as well as other Catholic Church leaders. The point here is how recent activities seem to be positioning a religious body toward the 'False Religion' of the End Times.

Interestingly, the word Catholic means 'all embracing', and from a church standpoint, it represents the 'universal church'. The Catholic faith has many ceremonies, dictated prayers to repeat, actions, and man-made laws that are not written in scripture. Worshiping or praying to Mary (Jesus rebuked - Luke 11:27-28), prayer to dead saints to take action for them (Peter rebuked - Acts 10:25-26), believing in second chances via Purgatory (Jesus controls who enters - Revelation 3:7), are but a few key points to call out. All of these are non-Biblical: In each situation, they point back to the only truth - the Word of God (John 1:14, 14:6)!

Catholic Church hierarchy reminds me of the Sadducees and Pharisees of Jesus's time; they held authority which was not to be questioned. This is very comparable to many Catholic Leadership positions, and the nearly unquestionable authority of their elected Pope. Today's truths show there is a need reign in their authority and sovereignty...they should be more accountable for their actions.

Let's explore that....Catholicism is a 'Christian' faith; yet, there are actions taken, or statements made by the current Pope (Francis 2013-current) that contradict what scripture teaches. Some of these are very subtle, while others are quite transparently acting in contention to scripture. This is a limited review, as there are more questionable references if one simply takes an unbiased look.

The Pope: Paving the way for the False Prophet

In many conversations, people refer to cult leaders as the potential false prophet instead of what they are; false Christs (Matthew 24:24). They claim to be a reincarnation of Christ, or the image of Christ, or speaking on behalf of God, as a new-age prophet. But this is simply a man, trying to make others believe they are a god.

The actual False Prophet in Revelation presents a much greater threat. This is someone that can influence through a religion that appears legitimate, even to some of God's faithful. This person will attack the very foundation of the church body - from the inside.

Graying the lines of religions: February 4, 2019, Pope Francis signed the Abu Dhabi agreement with Grand Imam of Al-Azhar (top Muslim cleric). The agreement states that Catholics and Muslims believe the same God, and that God wills a plurality of contradictory religions. Public Broadcast Station states this as blurring the lines.

What is missing is how Muslims view Jesus, the foundation of the Christian faith. It is impossible to remain obedient to the teachings of two religions with opposing views of the central figure of its faith (John 14:6, Acts 4:11-12).

On November 2013, Pope Francis stated, 'We must never forget that they (Muslim) profess to hold the faith of Abraham, and together with us they adore the one merciful God...'. In essence, this is the starting of a new religion, commonly referred to as Chrislam. Interestingly, this 'fictional religion' was referred to by Arthur C. Clark in his 1993 novel, *The Hammer Of God*, as the merging of Christian and Muslim faiths. Clark was ahead of his time in thinking outside of the box regarding religions.

Influencing education: September 12, 2020, Pope Francis announced a Global Compact for education, which has been campaigned since October 15, 2020. This would provide oversight (or influence) of the global curriculum for world education. This is greatly promoted by liberal left globalists who seek to influence people at a very young age.

There are many statements from Pope Francis that have raised eyebrows both within and outside of the Catholic Church. I will not state that the current Pope is the False Prophet; however, I have never seen a person in history that seems to be cast from that mold.

He admitted that the Catholic Church has hidden clerical abuse of nuns, and even sexual slavery (February 2019), which was shockingly transparent. He has been quite clear on his stance against abortion, to which conservatives offer 'kudos'. On the other side of the coin, here are a few comments that caught my eye...or ear.

Note: Please feel free to fact check; these are several publications offering these updates, so no one source is specifically referenced...

- April 2018, he stated that 'you don't have to believe or seek faith to go to Heaven, but people should obey their conscience, and God will forgive them' (Ephesians 2:8-9).
- August 2018, speaking at an LGBT conference on gender identity he stated 'Human identity is the choice of the individual, one that can change over time.' Given the audience/event, this seems to promote or at least that God would accept transgenderism (Genesis 1:27, 5:2, Matthew 19:4, Mark 10:6).
- June 2016, at Rome's Pastoral Congress, he spoke on cohabitation before marriage, saying, 'I've seen a lot of fidelity in these cohabitations, and I am sure that this is a real marriage... because of their fidelity.' This blurs the line of an official marriage. It seems 2 people can simply declare themselves married, and that's accepted by the Pope (1 Corinthians 7:9, 36).

- October 2014, he stated 'I loved every article ever written by Leonidas Barletta'. Leonidas is one of the well known members of the Argentine Communist Party (even confirmed by CIA).
- September 2017, while at a luncheon, someone asked how to reason with an atheist, and he said, 'Look, the last thing you must do is say anything.' Really? I would beg to differ (Ephesians 4:15).
- March 2018, he is asked if bad souls are punished and he replied, 'There is no hell, there is the disappearance of sinful souls.' Kind of throws judgement out the window doesn't it? I guess if you are bad.. you just disappear (Revelation 20:15)?
- April 2013, he writes, 'Jewish people can no longer be accused of having killed God, as they were for a long time. When one reads the account of the passion, it is clear.' The Pope is attempting to change scripture's teachings (Acts 2:36, Matthew 27:24-25).
- June 2013, regarding confession, he says, 'We look to Jesus Christ and say, this is your sin, and I will sin again. And Jesus likes that, because it was His mission: to become the sinner for us, to liberate us.' What about repentance? So, we can just sin as much as we want and keep coming back to confession (Hebrews 10:26)?
- July 2013, at a press conference, he says, 'If someone is gay and he searches for the Lord and has good will, who am I to judge.' Jesus has already judged their lifestyle choice (Revelation 21:8).
- December 2019, 'We need other maps, other paradigms that might help us to change our ways of thinking. We are not in Christianity, not anymore!'. All I can say is, 'wow' (1 John 2:18-4:6).

The point here is, there are many statements that the current Pope has made that gray the lines of God's Word. This only casts doubt on scripture and creates division within the church. False teaching is shown by appealing to man instead of staying faithful to scripture.

Technology - Paving the way for one world Currency

The World Health Organization (WHO) has asked the world to stop using physical money for fear this may spread Coronavirus. Instead, they are pushing for entirely cashless environment, and encouraging digital means of payment. This could also be used to track each man, woman, and child's actions... anywhere. (Big brother anyone?)

This would be controlled by some type of technology, potentially digital currency like SDR (which has been ready for public use since 2018), but most likely a chip or something similar to this. This effort is being pushed by the ID2020 Alliance, who is working closely with the UN. This 'ID' is being considered a fundamental human right, and there will be no discrimination as to who will be able to receive this ID.

The best environment for this to become possible would be for the world's monetary system to crash. We are seeing poverty in all areas of the world. Coronavirus has caused businesses to close, people to lose their jobs and income. Growing conflicts have led to looting, rioting, and anarchy that is literally burning businesses to the ground. All of this creates a financial burden, and brings the world closer and closer to a total economic system collapse, or at least faltering to the point where change is demanded.

An economic collapse could be started with one well-placed Electro-Magnetic Pulse (EMP) from a nuclear explosion (higher altitude = larger range). This has the ability to disable (if not destroy) every electronic device in its range - everything would 'go dark'. No phones, internet, computers, lights, utilities, automobiles, airplanes and more...all rendered unusable. That's a scary scenario; yet, a very realistic scenario.

And other technologies are also being developed...

Case and point

Microsoft has a pending patent #WO/2020/060606. This would implement a system in which people are assigned tasks to be completed. This 'monitor' (specified as 'smart technology') would confirm task completion, and then pay the individual with 'cryptocurrencies' instead of money. Then what? They could use that cryptocurrency to purchase what they need via their 'monitor' being scanned at the register.

Once the chip is in place, this would become the 'normal' way to confirm individual identify. 'Chips' are currently being used by some corporations (placed under the skin) instead of ID badges. Much like the cryptocurrency above, this could also be programmed with financial information so that it could be used to purchase anything (like a debit card right in our skin). Wouldn't it be interesting if the choices for this chip would be in the forehead or the right hand (Revelation 13:16-17)?

How about another option... from Bill Gates again??

December 2019: This is interesting timing - remember Coronavirus had not even occurred yet, or at least not confirmed. Bill Gates started a strong push for technology called the 'quantum dot tattoo' to ID vaccinated kids. This tattoo would not be seen, but would glow under infrared light. The information embedded in the tattoo could be read by a portable device, such as a cell phone.

Incredibly, this process is made possible by using an artificial enzyme called 'luciferase' (Lucifer-ase). It was hard not to laugh when I researched this...it's almost too obvious, isn't it? Okay - so enough on that...let's look at some other events...

The last 60-70 years has been just an explosion of events that seem to further position us for the End Times...

Other prominent events to consider...

- Israel's return (1948-curr) (Matthew 24:32-33)
- Famines, pestilence, disease (Matthew 24:7)
- Rebuilding of Temple (Ezekiel 40-48, Matthew 24:15)
- Believers growing cold (Matthew 24:12, Revelation 3:16)
- Rumors of Wars / Natural disasters (Matthew 24:6-8)
- Gospel shared globally (Matthew 24:14)
- Many False Christs (cults, etc.) (Matthew 24:23-26)
- False teachers deceiving many (Matthew 24:11, 24)
  Including within the Christian church
  Witchcraft/Satanic Church (growing acceptance)
- Christian persecution (Matthew 24:9-10)
- Defunding Police/Authority (2 Peter 2:10, 3:3)
  Marxism/Far-left liberalism (1 Timothy 4; 6:3-5)
- Israel/Arab initial peace treaties (prep for Daniel 9:27)
- History skewed, truth is biased (2 Timothy 4:4)

Jesus said that the generation that sees these things will not die until all of these things are fulfilled (Matthew24:34). This is why I believe these things will continue to grow in frequency and intensity, and then Christ will return.

People who are not watching for this will continue life like normal, and they will be surprised, and miss out on His return before the Tribulation (Matthew 24:38-42, 25:1-13). The recent peace treaties forged under Donald Trump's administration could be laying the foundation for the seven year peace treaty, penned by the Beast to start the Tribulation period (Daniel 9:27)!

Do you recognize the signs of the times?

Conclusion

Do you find any of this interesting? Do you consider all of this to be a coincidence, or perhaps you consider this to be just another conspiracy theory? Maybe you've decided to keep turning the pages out of sheer amusement to see what this 'crazy author' comes up with next? Whatever your thoughts may be, I'll let you come to your own conclusions on all of this.

One more reminder. I don't want you to take this writing as absolute truth. As I stated, the only absolute truth is the Word of God (John 17:17). I want to encourage you to take this writing as a starting point for your own personal studies. If you have any interest in the topics that have been discussed here, do your research, open discussions with others, and always seek truth.

As a Christian, I am accountable for my own choices, and joyfully passing on the truth of scripture. There is no further burden on me, except to share the Gospel message when the opportunity arises. You are the only one that is accountable for your eternal future; so that is where we will conclude...

Chapter 10
Your personal salvation...

eader, I am now speaking directly to you. The truth is, there have been several people that have claimed we are entering the End Times throughout history. I want to be clear to state that I am not offering any specific date that this may occur. In fact, anyone that is attempting to sell a date that any of these events will begin, is acting directly against the teaching of Jesus (Matthew 24:36).

No person knows when they could be taking their last breath in this lifetime. Any of us could suffer a physical health issue, or be involved in an accident that is fatal. That is, and always has been the delicate and finite life of human beings. That is not me trying to spread fear, panic, or being morbid - that is reality.

The real question for you: Where do you think you would end up if that did occur? Your answer is going to be based on what you believe to be truth. Views will differ based on whether you believe in God, a different religious doctrine or theistic view, or if you are an Agnostic, or Atheist.

Some people believe that our individual lives are all there is or ever will be; so we should make the most of it (1 Corinthians 15:32). Then when we die, we simply decompose into the earth. People can buy into this because you can dig up graves and see the bodies that have been, or are in the process of decomposing. However, this process is natural and falls in line with Biblical teaching of our human bodies. This is to be expected...remember the dry bones coming to life?

Others believe in reincarnation, which states that a person is born as an everlasting soul into a vessel. When that vessel dies (physical death), that soul is reborn into a new vessel (could be just about anything - person, plant, thing). This 'rebirth' falls in line with Christian teaching; however, we do not become another thing on earth. Our soul is immediately in Abraham's Bosom/Paradise while we await Christ's return at the Rapture (Luke 16:22, Luke 23:43). Also note, Luke was a medical doctor, so he spoke of many things in the physical aspect... something to consider when he is speaking of our soul's dwelling place after physical death.

Muslims also believe in one God, Allah. In death, the body is separated from the soul and transferred to the afterlife. What happens to that soul afterward is debated among Muslim theologians. That said, you must believe in the afterlife, for it is one of the six articles of the Muslim faith. It is agreed though, that they are judged based on good or bad deeds; works vs. grace.

The truth is, religious options are almost limitless...

The biggest difference in the religions of the world comes down to how you view the major characters. Buddha, Mohammed, God the Father, Allah, Jesus, Zeus, Satan, etc., and the laws or rules they have bestowed on humans. There is a lot of variety, even within each belief, which can make all of this quite confusing. I want to encourage you to study world religions long term, which can help us to approach religious differences with more respect and love. Many religions call their god a 'god of love and peace'; the Christian faith is no different. Christians are suppose to lead with love and grace, in appreciation that those has been given to us as well (Ephesians 3:2, 1 Peter 4:10).

If this topic of study piques your interest, I would suggest you speak with religious leaders that you trust. Also, study the differing faiths on your own, and then ask questions... but *definitely*, ask the questions. Confirm what is taught in two ways: Through the scripture they claim to adhere to (misquotes, or statements taken out of context happen quite often); and then challenge information with the Holy Bible.

Why the Bible? The Bible has never (and I do mean N-E-V-E-R) been proven wrong. It is the source of truth (John 17:17), manifested in the man Jesus Christ (John 1:14, 14:6); for our understanding of His ways, and correction in our lives (2 Timothy 3:16).

The authentication of the Bible has been on trial for many years (1 Corinthians 1:25). Ironically, science is forced to go against its own laws (thermodynamics for starters) to try to explain the existence of anything to be honest. Simply stated, "you can't get something from nothing". But that double-standard doesn't stop them from trying.

Whether you study or not, I want to get back to the reality of our lives today. You do not know when you will die, and I would warn everyone against the attitude of "I'm not going to worry about it".

Most of us have experienced the loss of someone we know - that is life. Human bodies are fragile (regardless of physical strength), and our time is limited by mortality - that is reality.

Although religions differ in many ways, there is a commonality among them. There is reward or punishment for each individual's works in some form; but depending on the faith, the consequences can range from non-essential, to eternal suffering. Again - that is not to scare - it is reality. Here's a simple question...

Why do you believe what you believe?

Okay, on second thought, maybe that's not that simple... But, this question is part of who you are. It is your faith, it defines moral character, it is what you deem to be reality in the world we live in today. It is truly one of the most important questions you can answer when it comes to who you really are.

After all of my years of study, I have not found anything that disproves the Christian faith. Biblical teaching conflicts with worldly teachings; challenges are to be expected, as shown in the previous chapter. In all situations, when I have relied on the Bible as my source of truth, it has succeeded. My understanding is not God's (by any means). My faith is in His Word, and His finished victory over death and sin at Calvary: Freedom for all who believe in the Lord Jesus Christ (1 Corinthians 15:55-57).

This faith has not only allowed me to feel confident in my eternal well-being, but has helped me through many of life's toughest situations. Death of loved ones, struggles with worldly lusts, pride, people pleasing, and even with my own significance on this planet. We all struggle to find out who we are, and the significant meaning in our lives.

The truth will set you free

As we stated in the previous chapter, truth is reality and it is NOT subjective. There is simply no getting around that. If someone does not see the truth or reality, their perception is skewed and should be corrected. We need a baseline for that correction, and as stated, that is the Holy Bible.

So here is the truth. Every single human being on the planet is a sinner. The Bible is clear that this does not change because of your personal beliefs, culture, or any physical characteristics: All have sinned and fallen short of the glory of God (Romans 3:23). So what does that mean for mankind?

When God created the world, there was no need to tend to anything. Everything grew, and there was no death; this is why people refer to the Garden of Eden as a desired 'perfection'. Even when God created Adam and Eve, there was no sin, no death, not even the need to work for their food, water, etc. Nothing was needed or desired, until the Devil tempted Eve, and she persuaded Adam to eat from the Tree of the Knowledge of Good and Evil (Genesis 3)...the 'forbidden fruit'.

So, sin entered the world through man (Adam - Genesis 3:6). This meant that creation was now cursed by God (Genesis 3:17), and death entered creation (Romans 5:12-21). Mankind would now need to work for their food and to preserve the planet, for all things now die (Genesis 3:19). Sin is in our flesh, of all men, yesterday, today, and through the Millennial Kingdom. It will remain until the old Heaven and old Earth are passed away (Revelation 21:1).

I also want to be clear about the death that is referred to here, for there are two deaths. One is physical, and the other is spiritual. This is a key to understanding salvation...

The First Death - Physical Death

Physical death is temporary. This will be experienced by every human (Hebrews 9:27); unless they are a Believer that is 'caught up' to meet Jesus in the clouds at the time of the Rapture (1 Thessalonians 4:17). It should also be noted that physical death will continue through the Millennium (Isaiah 65:20, Revelation 20:14). This is reality.

The Second Death - Spiritual Death

Spiritual death is eternal. This is what is referred to when Believers celebrate their 'victory over death' (1 Corinthians 15:51-57). Our faith frees us from this punishment for our sins (Revelation 2:11). The second death is the ultimate judgement for non-Believers (Revelation 20:11-15) who have rejected Jesus as their Savior. They will be found guilty of their sins, and tossed into the Lake of Fire.

No Believer will face the second death. (Revelation 20:6)

Today is the Day!

You may be reading this and thinking, 'I don't have to worry about that stuff, I'm not even close to death'. Luke covered this as well (Luke 12:19). I will restate this again, you do not know when you will die. Although you can avoid getting into life-threatening situations, you cannot avoid accidents. And, there is no second chance...

When you die, you will be accountable for the choices you have made of your free will during your life. Second chances are false teaching, false hope, and a one way ticket to the Lake of Fire. One life - one chance - reality.

Christian living

There are many verses to refer to here. My concern though, is that you may also hear of the 'restrictions' of Christian living and think... how boring. But I would also challenge this with what you are being told. Review the Holy Bible to see what it teaches. Here is a quick example that is often taught incorrectly to people.

A person can have an alcoholic drink, even attend parties, but should do so as Christians. Jesus sat at the table many times with 'publicans' and 'sinners' so that he could model holy living, and share His light through the Gospel message. He attended the wedding in Cana and turns the water into wine (John 2:1-11). Not only that, it was considered 'good' wine by worldly standards (John 2:10). The drink isn't the problem - it's the intention of the heart that is the issue (Hebrews 4:12).

It *IS* sinning however, if your intention on drinking is to get drunk (Galatians 5:21). No drunken person will enter into Heaven (1 Corinthians 6:10); however, one who has been drunk can be forgiven when the sin is confessed in faith. We see Noah as an example when he was drunk and accidentally uncovered his naked body while passed out (Genesis 9:21). Yet, he is considered a great man of faith!

The point is, becoming a Christian doesn't mean you can never touch a glass of wine again, can't have fun, or that you won't stumble or even fall down on your faith walk. In reality, becoming a Christian is a changing of the heart, which drives the actions of our lives (Galatians 5:22-23).

Our actions are driven by intentions, that is what must change. If we have a lifestyle, an addiction, issues with pride, and worldly desires, those are accepted and pursued by the intentions of our heart. That must change.

If we do not change, we will continue to pursue those things. That pursuit will be the fruit of our works, and as we have said, that will not 'buy' our salvation. At the Great White Throne, those works will be judged and unworthy, and that person will be tossed into the Lake of Fire. That is reality.

This is why my 'life verse' is Hebrews 4:12:

For the word of God is alive and active. Sharper than any double-edged sword, it penetrates even to dividing soul and spirit, joints and marrow; it judges the thoughts and attitudes of the heart.

How to accept Jesus Christ and be saved

This is truly the key, and again, is sometimes misunderstood as compared to what scripture teaches us. For you and I, today, there is only one way to Heaven, and that is through believing in Jesus Christ (John 3:16). So, that's pretty simple, right? You just believe that Jesus Christ existed, that He is the Son of God, died for our sins, and is in Heaven preparing a place for us... right?

No. That is not all there is to it. The angels that were in Heaven know all of this, and accept this as reality; yet, they shudder because they know they are damned to the Lake of Fire for all eternity (James 2:19). But keep reading in James, for he shows that faith (belief) without works is dead (James 2:20). But always remember, works without faith is dead as well (Ephesians 2:8-9).

Once you accept who Jesus is, you must then hand your life to Him and His will. This means you open your mind and heart in every way, confessing your sins and asking forgiveness for them, and repenting from them. Turning your life over to gaining understanding of what God wants you to do in this life, and dedicating your efforts to His glory alone. That is true salvation through faith!

Conforming to God's Will as a Christian

Once saved, you have started a new journey. The old man (worldly life) has died, and the new man (Christian) is living (Romans 6:6-23). This is the beginning, the new life includes a new mind that now needs to conform to the Christian way of living (Romans 12:2).

You must continue to grow in your understanding of what His will is. Reading His Word, attending church and having discussions with mature Christians, prayer and abstaining from worldly desires, lusts, etc. This will lead to cleaner living, cleaner conscience, and sober thinking. There is great joy in being a Christian, great appreciation for the freedom from sin, and great confidence in our eternal future with God!

But there's even more... We still have to live in the world, right? This crazy world we live in still relies on money for food, shelter, transportation, which means we need jobs. We all want to succeed, and be recognized for good work, and that *SHOULD* continue. Being a Christian doesn't mean you now brush off the rest of the world, but instead you take on the world with integrity.

This starts at home. As individuals, we are simply accountable for our actions, but we are still children of our parents and we should respect them (Exodus 21:17, Ephesians 6:1-3). And as we become married, we need to take on the roles and responsibilities of being a husband or wife (Ephesians 5:22-33). And then, we may end up facing one of the greatest challenges of our lives...parenting!

As parents, we must teach our children what is good, and what is right in life. We must not provoke them to anger (Ephesians 6:4). And we are to guide and nurture them, correcting with love and kindness, but firmly. Again, this brings us back to our playbook in life... the Bible (2 Timothy 3:16).

To broaden this even wider... In our work, we are to respect those in authority over us (Ephesians 6:5, 1 Peter 2:18), regardless of the position, or job title we hold. Also, if we are leaders, teachers, or elders, we have great accountability (James 3:1). We should avoid threatening actions toward those we have authority over; instead, providing encouragement, and the tools they need to succeed (Colossians 4:1, Ephesians 6:9).

And even broader... We are to respect the laws of the land which we are in (currently) by understanding God has put every leader in place (Romans 13). Each country, each business, each home, and each room is filled with many experiences, opportunities, and challenges. The point is - whatever we do, we should give 110% effort with our whole heart, to produce the best result we can (Colossians 3:23).

These actions, these 'works', they come from your changed heart; your desire to do God's will. These works are the Fruit of the Spirit (Galatians 5:22-23) that we mentioned earlier. By doing these, you please God, but you will also gain respect for your integrity from other people (Proverbs 14:22-32). They may even ask you why you are the way you are... now you can answer them with confidence. Hey, maybe you'll even have the opportunity to share the Gospel, and save someone else from the second death in the process. I truly hope you do.

Thank you for reading, and I hope this has provoked some thoughts, spurred questions, and created some points to consider in your own life. Each of our lives is very challenging, which is why we need a strong foundation to stand on. That foundation is the Bible, and our personal devotion to Jesus.

"But as for me and my house, we will serve the Lord."
Joshua 24:15

I wish blessings on you today and always, in the love and grace of our Lord and Savior, Jesus Christ. Amen.

About the Author

Bobby is, first and foremost, a Christian family man and friend to many. He has earned a Bachelor's Degree in Business Management, as well as certifications for Project Management and Accounting. Currently, he is a corporate Critical Situation Manager for North America, public speaker, certified coach, and seasoned mentor.

Most of his time is spent with Corporate Leadership courses, Community Leadership engagement, Life Coaching for peers and colleagues, and working with adult and teenage Recovery programs. In his free time, he is a passionate entertainer. He has 'dabbled' in film, music, stage, and writing, as well as volunteering at his local church in Minnesota as a worship leader, and teacher in Adult Education classes. Bobby has been a music teacher on and off for over 15 years, focused primarily on guitar.

Music is, and forever will be one of Bobby's greatest passions, having written and performed for over 30 years. In 2010, he was offered a record contract; however, through prayer and discussions with his wife, it was not the right time. Instead, he invested his resources into creating a home studio, in which he has written and produced over 50 original works, and recorded several projects for others.

In 2018, he founded Faith In Family Films, LLC (FIFF) in Minnesota, and has a distributed film through PureFlix and 60+ countries with Amazon Global. The focus of FIFF is to create faith-based, family-friendly products, that avoid simulated intimacy, nudity, and extreme profanity. This was yet another calling to battle worldly morals and attitudes that are prominent in the TV and film industry.

2020 has had its own set of challenges for everyone. Coronavirus (Covid-19) created situations of isolation, and promoted working from home for many people. Bobby saw this as an opportunity to use that time to self-reflect, and put more time into writing. His heart drove him to look at his life, his faith, the world around him, and where it all seems to be heading. This book is the fruit of that review; hopefully, the first of many to come.

Blessings, today and always,
in the name of Jesus Christ...

References

1. Schuyler, E. (1976). The Pilgrim Study Bible. (1st ed.). United States of America: Oxford University Press, Inc. Strong, J. (1997). Strong's Exhaustive Concordance. Hendrickson.

2. *Bible hub: Search, read, study the bible in many languages.* (n.d.). Biblehub.Com. Retrieved January 5, 2021, from http://biblehub.com

3. *Read & study the Bible - daily verse, Scripture by topic, stories.* (n.d.). Biblestudytools.Com. Retrieved January 5, 2021, from http://biblestudytools.com

4. *OpenBible.info.* (n.d.). Openbible.Info. Retrieved January 5, 2021, from http://openbible.info

5. Stoner, P. (1976). Science Speaks. (Revised ed.). United States of America: Moody Press.

6. *Bible: Scofield Brevier Reference Bible* (1917th ed.). (1983). Oxford University Press.

7. Ryrie, C. .C. (1977). Dispensationalism Today. (17th ed.). United States of America: The Moody Bible Institute of Chicago.

8. Webster, N. (2017). An American dictionary of the English language: Intended to exhibit, I. the origin, affinities and primary signification of English words, as far as they have been ascertained. II. The genuine orthography and pronunciation of words, according to general U. Andesite Press.

9. *Temple Institute.* (2020, January 9). Templeinstitute.Org. https://templeinstitute.org/

10. *Home.* (n.d.). Jewsforjesus.Org. Retrieved January 5, 2021, from https://jewsforjesus.org/

11. Wells, H. .G. (1940). The New World Order. (1st ed.). Australia: Secker & Warburg.

12. CDC. (2021, January 5). *CDC Works 24/7*. Cdc.Gov. https://www.cdc.gov/

13. *Home*. (n.d.). Who.Int. Retrieved January 5, 2021, from https://www.who.int/

14. JHCHS website designer. (2020, December 11). *Event 201*. Centerforhealthsecurity.Org. https://www.centerforhealthsecurity.org/event201/

15. (N.d.). Worldgovernmentsummit.Org. Retrieved January 5, 2021, from https://www.worldgovernmentsummit.org/

16. United Nations. (n.d.). United Nations | Peace, dignity and equality on a healthy planet. Retrieved January 5, 2021, from https://www.un.org/en/

17. *"Chrislam" Combines Christian and Muslim Beliefs*. (n.d.). Pbs.Org. Retrieved January 5, 2021, from https://www.pbs.org/newshour/extra/daily-videos/chrislam-combines-christian-and-muslim-beliefs/

18. Clarke, A. C. (1995). *The hammer of god*. Orbit.

19. Identity2020 Systems, Inc, a registered 501c, & Identity2020 Systems, Inc, a registered 501c. (2019, February 26). *ID2020*. Id2020.Org. https://id2020.org/alliance

20. Abramson, D., Fu, D., & Johnson, J. E., Jr. (2020). Cryptocurrency system using body activity data (Patent No. 2020060606:A1). In *World Patent* (2020060606:A1).

21. *Bill Gates funds invisible quantum tattoo hidden in Coronavirus vaccine for storing vaccination history*. (2020, September 7). Greatgameindia.Com. https://greatgameindia.com/invisible-tattoo-coronavirus-vaccine/

The Times

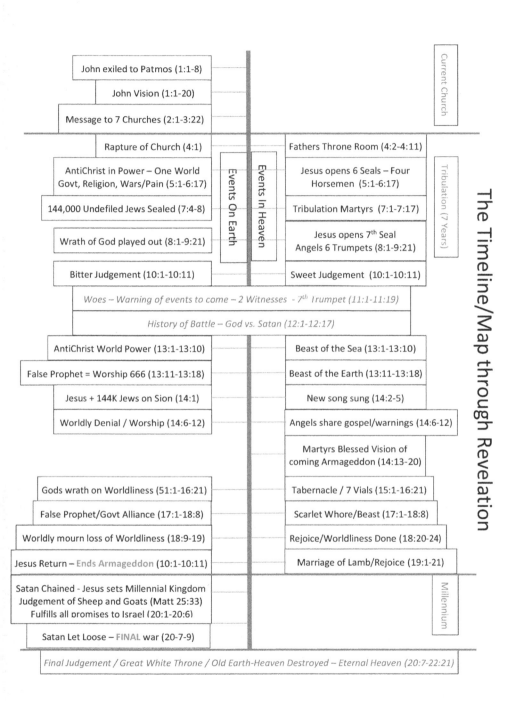

John exiled to Patmos (1:1-8)

John Vision (1:1-20)

Message to 7 Churches (2:1-3:22)

Events On Earth	Events In Heaven
Rapture of Church (4:1)	Fathers Throne Room (4:2-4:11)
AntiChrist in Power – One World Govt, Religion, Wars/Pain (5:1-6:17)	Jesus opens 6 Seals – Four Horsemen (5:1-6:17)
144,000 Undefiled Jews Sealed (7:4-8)	Tribulation Martyrs (7:1-7:17)
Wrath of God played out (8:1-9:21)	Jesus opens 7th Seal Angels 6 Trumpets (8:1-9:21)
Bitter Judgement (10:1-10:11)	Sweet Judgement (10:1-10:11)

Woes – Warning of events to come – 2 Witnesses - 7th Trumpet (11:1-11:19)

History of Battle – God vs. Satan (12:1-12:17)

AntiChrist World Power (13:1-13:10)	Beast of the Sea (13:1-13:10)
False Prophet = Worship 666 (13:11-13:18)	Beast of the Earth (13:11-13:18)
Jesus + 144K Jews on Sion (14:1)	New song sung (14:2-5)
Worldly Denial / Worship (14:6-12)	Angels share gospel/warnings (14:6-12)
	Martyrs Blessed Vision of coming Armageddon (14:13-20)
Gods wrath on Worldliness (51:1-16:21)	Tabernacle / 7 Vials (15:1-16:21)
False Prophet/Govt Alliance (17:1-18:8)	Scarlet Whore/Beast (17:1-18:8)
Worldly mourn loss of Worldliness (18:9-19)	Rejoice/Worldliness Done (18:20-24)
Jesus Return – Ends Armageddon (10:1-10:11)	Marriage of Lamb/Rejoice (19:1-21)

Satan Chained - Jesus sets Millennial Kingdom Judgement of Sheep and Goats (Matt 25:33) Fulfills all promises to Israel (20:1-20:6)

Satan Let Loose – FINAL war (20-7-9)

Final Judgement / Great White Throne / Old Earth-Heaven Destroyed – Eternal Heaven (20:7-22:21)

Current Church

Tribulation (7 Years)

Millennium

The Timeline/Map through Revelation

NOTES:

NOTES:

Made in the USA
Monee, IL
09 May 2021